Year of the Whore

STEVE BALDERSON

DIKENGA BOOKS

Copyright © 2023. All rights reserved.

www.dikenga.com

ISBN: 978-1-7354569-9-7

ABRIDGED EDITION

For the warriors.

CONTENTS

1
Grazie Mille

Arriving in Venice is done by speedboat—as mysterious and thrilling as a Bond film—and we rocketed across the lagoon between Venezia and the airport, eventually nearing the celebrated constellation of islands. Our boat slowed as we entered the famous canals, narrowing at every turn that slid us deeper into the ancient labyrinth and mystery that is Venice.

Ornate *palazzos* and decorative buildings lined the canals, towering over us. As the sun set and a fog settled in, the purple of night was fast descending. The three of us were delirious from transatlantic travel. After a brief dinner, we returned to our rooms and collapsed into sleep.

I woke the next morning to the sounds of church bells. There seemed to be thousands of them, echoing from every direction. I opened the enormous windows and leaned out into the air, so crisp and fresh. The bells marked the start of the hour and had no intention of stopping anytime soon. I grabbed my phone to record their sounds and use them in the soundtrack for a future movie I'll direct. It was a cacophony of exquisite chimes and tones.

My partner of 12 years, who I'll call "Bernie," was an emotionally abusive sociopath, and I don't use these terms lightly. We were life partners as well as business partners. We weren't married, thank God, because same-sex marriage wasn't yet legal. My brother coined the name "Bernie," because like Bernie Madoff who stole from tens of thousands of people with his infamous Ponzi scheme, my partner Bernie—I discovered too late—stole money from me and my family. Lots of it. This theft was profoundly unethical, the very definition of stealth, but alas—not against the law. I could do nothing except flee. And I did.

After Bernie's betrayal, I felt utterly broken—psychologically, spiritually, physically. Any dreams of intimacy or sexuality had long since passed and were now dormant. More like six feet under.

While healing and grieving, my mother gave me the best advice. She told me quite seriously, "We come from a long line of warriors... Cut off our feet... and we'll learn how to walk."

As a child, my mother protected herself by hiding in a locked bathroom when my abusive alcoholic grandfather came after her with a butcher's knife. She grew up a warrior and raised me to be a warrior.

For my 40th birthday, I knew I needed to celebrate my new freedom, my life, my future. Hell, I needed time to even imagine a future. I planned a vacation to Venice for the entire month of January. My friends Jennifer and

Erin joined me. I scored an off-season discounted rate at an exquisite four-star hotel near *Piazza San Marco*. The hotel was just steps away from the magnificent *Basilica di San Marco*, with its domes and golden mosaic interior, and *Palazzo Ducale* (The Doge's Palace), a masterpiece of medieval architecture that looks like a cake. A deliciously Gothic 12th-century cake.

I opened a gay social hook up app to find out who might be both gay and nearby. I'm a big fan of the apps because they allow people to basically be screened before ever meeting in person. I usually message a guy who appears interesting in one way or another, and if he wants to meet up, I'll agree to meeting him in public for a coffee. If the guy is unwilling to meet in public, I delete the conversation. Guys who refuse to meet in public are either married, not out, not actually the person in the photos, a serial killer stalking prey, or possibly a bigoted homophobic gang wanting to harm gay people.

I love that the app totally abolishes the need to go to a bar in order to meet someone. Sure, it's a bit like ordering food from a delivery menu, or looking through headshots before deciding who to audition, but it saves a lot of valuable time. Sexually, I'm a total top. Imagine spending all night with someone learning you have amazing chemistry in every way until it comes down to it and you learn he's also a total top. The app lets you sidestep a lot of the bullshit no one enjoys about the dating process.

I came across a profile for a man named Antonio and after a discussion, we decided to meet for a coffee. Jennifer and Erin sat nearby, as backup, in case Antonio turned out to be a nightmare. In the distance, I saw him hurrying down the tiny street.

Antonio, a northern, blonde-haired, blue-eyed Italian, wore clothing made of the finest fabric, a grey cashmere scarf, and a dark wool overcoat. Through all the layers of clothing he seemed strong and well-proportioned. He looked like a university professor straight out of central casting. I learned he was working on his dissertation in Art History and taught calligraphy in his spare time. He was dashing, smart, polite, affectionate and I admired his kindness. Plus, his blue eyes mesmerized me.

After our coffee, I introduced him to my friends and he offered to show us around Venice. Though I was disappointed that Antonio and I wouldn't be immediately fooling around, I was also eager to explore more than just his body.

That afternoon he showed me, Jennifer, and Erin, the Venice only locals knew. We walked a block or two off the main tourist street to a hidden gem of a bar frequented by the locals. They served *cicchetti*—the Italian version of tapas. We shared spicy olives, toasts topped with spec and cheese, and sipped delightfully dry white wine.

The next day, Antonio took me to lunch at a hidden spot, and when we entered, he spoke familiarly with the hostess. We were ushered into the back room where a different menu was served for workmen on their lunch hour. I devoured the experience. Incredibly inexpensive (and excellent) wine, some of the best pasta I've ever had in my life and sitting next to me was a guy who I couldn't believe was actually real. We flirted and under the table I leaned my leg against his. His affection and kindness radiated in all directions. I wanted him to kiss me. Yet, he didn't.

After two weeks of Antonio joining me and my friends

for *prosecco* and *cicchetti*, I was becoming a bit restless. Antonio and I hadn't even made out yet. I'm from Kansas, so I don't know the customary dating or hook up etiquette involving gay Venetian guys, but I had assumed it would be more provocative or racy, more unabashed and immediate somehow. Finally, I decided to confront him.

"Antonio," I said, "We aren't dating. I don't live here. I'm going to leave Italy and return to the US soon. If we're going to fool around, we need to get this show on the road." He turned to me and leaned in close. I could feel his breath on my face, smell his soap and feel the warmth from his body.

"I think you're ready," he whispered. I immediately saw that Italian machismo cliché, and in my mind, I rolled my eyes. But it turns out desire is a treasure, and there was nothing cliché about Antonio. I'd been hungry to kiss him, to taste him, for weeks. Sitting close and feeling the brush of his leg against mine added to the slow burn.

Desire is, of course, something just out of reach and something not easy to grab. Something seemingly unattainable. And not being able to have it made me want it even more. An eruption was inevitable. Maybe it was part of his plan to feed my longing past the point of reasonable thought.

By the time we climbed the stairs to the top of the *palazzo* and entered his place, I had let go of all restraint. I kissed him, twisting my tongue around his. My fingers clumsily undid the top button of his shirt. I almost tore open his shirt to send the buttons flying across the room. But suddenly Antonio pulled back, leaving me panting, hungry, and a bit confused.

"Wait," he said.

Antonio paused, closed his eyes, and took several deep breaths. I waited but he was clearly in no hurry. If anything, he was slowing down. He patted his hair down, tucking strands behind his ears. Then slowly looked up at me. He leaned closer, speaking in a soft and low voice. "Now, we'll have sex. But I'd like you to think about each of the five senses—one sense at a time. Focus what you see, and... what you hear... and touch, and smell... and taste." His Italian accent lingered in the air.

I suddenly felt self-conscious, or somehow exposed. His stare was intense, unflinching. Was he seeing me—or was he looking right through me? I felt utterly transparent, like he could see into my heart, what I felt, and what I thought. It was wonderful and nerve-racking. I know I was desperate to be seen, really seen and accepted—for who I was. My ex never accepted or showed any interest in me. With Bernie it had been all business, cold and surface, nothing sensual or kind. And I felt like Antonio could see that. See me. I shuddered.

"First," he continued, "take in everything that you see. Soak up everything visual you can. The colors of the ceiling, that painting over there. Every bit of light from the Murano glass chandelier. Take it all in." He leaned in so close to my neck, I could feel his breath. I shivered. I wanted him to touch me, bite me, tear into me with his teeth. But he hovered. "Explore every shadow my body makes as it moves," he whispered. His voice was caring, gentle. "See the way my veins look along the muscles on my arm. How these wispy hairs move around my nipples in waves." He touched himself there, running his fingers lightly over his right nipple, then his left. "Watch my hands glide across my body. Take it in."

"I want to touch you," I said, and could feel my mouth watering. He took my hand and ran it through the treasure trail of hair running down the center of his chest and his defined stomach. The man was all muscle.

"How many colors do you see in my eyes?" he asked. "Green and gold and black and white? More? Tell me what you see."

I looked into his eyes, deeply, directly, and saw a kaleidoscope of color. To my surprise, just the act of looking so closely, the intimacy of it, caused a stirring in me.

"Green," I told him. "Gold, yellow, orange. Green."

"You said green already," he said, lifting my hand to his lips and sucking two of my fingers into his mouth. Gentle but unmistakable.

"What do you hear?" he asked. He leaned in and whispered in my ear, "Really listen to everything you can. Allow your ears to swim into my body. Hear my heartbeat. Hear yours. Tell me."

I could feel his warm breath on my ear, my neck. My nipples tingled.

"I hear your breath," I said. He blew into my ear, slow and soft, and I moaned, my heart racing.

"What else?"

"I hear my voice. The sounds of my breath and yours," I said.

"What do you hear when I do this?" he asked, slipping his hand into my pants and grabbing my now-throbbing dick. I gasped.

"Yes, that's right. I hear you, too, surprised and wanting. I like the way you sound when I touch you." He began to delicately trace the length of my dick, using his other hand to slide my pants down.

"Listen to every sound you can. Focus on hearing, despite what I'm doing down here. Listen to the sounds outside. Hear the seagulls?" Right then the cathedral bells started to ring at the top of the hour.

"Yes," he smiled wryly, "the bells. Do they ring for us? For the music we're making with our bodies?"

In my mind, I rolled my eyes again. If it wasn't for the sexy Italian accent, I would've told him to stop talking ten minutes ago.

He stepped away from me just far enough to strip off the rest of his clothes. As he pulled off his pants, my eyes widened. His physique was a total shock to me. Fully dressed he looked lean—don't must European men?—and maybe even thin. Or too thin. But underneath he was a different man altogether. All muscle, sinewy, strong, and coated with a clean layer of fur that gleamed in the light. How was that possible? His arms long ropes of muscle, his chest defined, a deep divide between his big square pecs, and all coated in a light brown fur. His stomach was lean, too, that classic V-shaped torso, his belly ribbed with muscle and a thick line of hair that led to his groin. My eyes were drawn away from his cock, sizable as it was, to his legs. Those, too, a wonder of muscle and hair, perfectly proportioned. Looking at him felt dream-like. *Is this the same guy? How can he look so different without his clothes?* He's transformed from ordinary-sexy to a beautiful, sensual God. I could hardly look at his cock, long and thick. I found myself panting, I had to close my eyes and take several breaths. *Yes, he is beauty itself. Now relax, open your eyes, take it all in.*

"Focus on what it feels like when I do this…" he said, leaning down into my lap and wrapping his lips around the head of my dick. The warmth and wetness made me tremble like the cathedral bells. I moaned, the sound surprising me it was so loud. I got chills along my skin. He lifted his mouth off me way too soon, then he ran his tongue up my chest and stood.

He took my hand in his, pressing it firmly to my chest, right at my heart. "Feel everything," he told me. "Feel it, savor it, appreciate it. There's no rush. Enjoy each moment of this, each sensation."

I glided my hand across his muscular chest, caressing him, my touch so light I felt like the hair on his chest was actually caressing me, the palm of my hand, my fingers. I could feel my dick pulsing, my breath shallow.

"Once you've fully focused everything you can feel, I want you to shift your focus to taste." As he removed the rest of my clothes, I tried to speak coherently, but my words came in fragments.

"Your mouth. So sweet," I said, tasting him. "Salty," I mumbled as I slid my tongue over his skin. Never in my life had I been verbal during sex. Most of my prior experiences were filled with either silence or grunts and rumbles.

He pushed me down on his bed, gently, firmly, but still wasn't giving me what I wanted. What my body was aching for.

"As you taste me, I want you to linger, smelling me. Breathe my scent into you," he said. His hands on the back of my head, he pulled me into his chest, his armpits, neck, even dropping his head down and pressing me into it so I could smell his hair.

I inhaled deeply.

"Tell me what you smell," he said.

"You smell delicious," I said, closing my eyes as I pushed my face back into his armpit. "You're spicy, fresh. I don't know how, but you smell like a campfire, too. Like the outdoors, like we're in the woods."

"Concentrate," he replied. "Concentrate as hard as you can. Take your time, Steve. We're not rushing toward anything. We're here, together. Go ahead, take me in."

What transpired was revolutionary for me. More than once I found myself surprised, stunned even, at the feelings that welled up inside me. Involuntary shudders, muscle spasms, tingles and waves of pure sexual adrenaline. It thrilled me, all of it, in ways a man had never thrilled me before. I felt that he was leading me, somehow, to feel my true nature, the nature of life itself. All my senses were awake and alive, crackling with sensation. For the first time in my life, I felt fully present, as if what we were doing was the only thing in the world, the only thing happening. The only thing that mattered. Each moment I felt something unexpected and fresh— the delightfully thick hair on his forearms, the soft skin of his thighs in contrast to the hard marble of muscle beneath it. With each discovery I thought, *Whoa, what is this!? What a marvel this is.*

Each time I got close to ejaculating, Antonio would shift what he was doing and refocus. Or we'd change positions, or locations, moving around the bedroom. He'd move us from the bed to an overstuffed brown leather chair next to the window, then toward a closet door embellished with speckled, old-fashioned mirrors. Building the desire to orgasm with a slow and intense fury. When I came, finally, I shot a massive load across the floor, my whole body shaking uncontrollably.

It took a long while to catch my breath and return to this planet, to his bedroom. I lay against his body, sweaty and slick, my chest heaving. Eventually I could feel his heart beating against the side of my body. I could still taste him on my tongue. His strong shoulders in my hands.

After a while (time was still a bit of a blur), we shared a cigarette. It was dusk and I stood naked at the floor-to-ceiling windows without a care in the world. The little standing balcony outside the glass had enough wrought iron scrollwork that, I figured, little was visible from across the canals. And if it was, I didn't care.

"Would you like some wine?" he asked, breaking the silence with his deep Italian accent, gentle but as ever fully in command.

I followed him into his kitchen. At that moment I realized he lived on the top floor of this old *palazzo*. Two bedrooms, three outdoor terraces, and enough *real* art to suggest there was more to his story. He was no ordinary calligraphy teacher.

We dressed and he walked me downstairs. I thought he'd say goodbye at the door, but instead he walked me back to my hotel. A gentlemanly gesture that I loved. His shoes clacking on the cobblestone streets. The steam from our breath in the air. I savored the taste of his sweetness on my lips and the sounds and smells all around us. When we reached the hotel, Antonio turned and said, in a most matter-of-fact voice, "Good job. I'll see you tomorrow. Meet me at the same time and place." He stared into my eyes, both of us smiling, then turned and walked away. No kiss goodbye. No hug. No handshake. The sound of his shoes on the cobblestone street, and a moment later he was gone.

I collapsed into bed whirling with pleasure. All my senses were on hyper drive. The soft Italian linens against my legs, the stability of the hotel bed and the firmness of the pillows are sensual luxuries I'll never forget. *Was the cliché about Europeans taking lovers and being great lovers, true? Or was I living in a dream?*

It suddenly occurred to me that the entire time I was with my ex, I had externalized my senses—all of them. My internal feeling and experiences had taken the back burner. I had been more dedicated to what the other person had, felt, and sensed. I had neglected my inner experience and sense of self for more than a decade.

That day and night in Venice woke me up. My spirit and soul had returned to my body. It was more than just sex. It was a new understanding and awareness of being alive. My senses flooded back into me with a spectacular roar.

At 15:00 the next day, I met Antonio at the corner café near his *palazzo*. We shared an espresso before making the long climb up the marble stairs to his penthouse.

"Now," he said, before I had the chance to seize him. "We're going to have sex, but what I'd like you to do this time is think about what you're doing and how you're doing it. And how your actions might affect my senses."

I traced every inch of his body with my tongue, slid my hands all over him. I listened to him whimper and moan as I twisted my tongue around, wondering what that must feel like, seeing what made him writhe, or hold still, or shiver. I could imagine how it felt, but I didn't know for sure.

My dick. Inside him. Thickened. Pulsed. Finally— shot deep.

He whimpered in heat and ejaculated at the same time I did. I wondered how he felt when I came inside him.

Could he feel each spurt? Could he feel the wetness of my semen, or maybe the throb of my dick? I wondered how I tasted to him, what I smelled like.

Paying close attention made me deliberately do things that I might not have otherwise done. Thinking about how he experienced my body, my touch, and my attention being focused to each present moment. I wasn't thinking about what would happen, or what had happened. My only focus was in each moment as it was happening. The now. This deep awareness of what was unfolding as it unfolded felt entirely new to me. A kind of super-presence that changed everything.

Conscious sex. That's another way to describe it. All the sex I'd had in the years prior now seemed totally unconscious. This new understanding and mindset— super-conscious.

Afterwards, standing alone on Antonio's balcony, savoring a cigarette, too, in new ways, I felt the loving embrace of Venice itself, twinkling in the twilight as darkness slowly fell.

"Very good," Antonio said from his place on the bed. "We'll meet again tomorrow."

I stared into his eyes, my face not a foot from his, as we stood in the *palazzo* the following day.

"What now?" I asked, my voice full of anticipation.

"Now," he said soothingly, "we're going to have sex." I liked the sound of that. I couldn't take my eyes off him. I wanted him. He continued, "I want you to combine all we've experienced and learned about each other. We will meld, no barriers to where you end and I begin. Only oneness. We'll combine our bodies and our senses at once, all together."

What followed was exhilarating. I visualized energy flowing around inside my body and spirit like a stream or river. I imagined this stream of energy flow through my hands, my tongue, my dick, and enter Antonio's body. Once inside him, I imagined the stream flowing around inside him before swimming back inside me. Back and forth.

At moments we did meld. And I couldn't tell where I ended, and he began, or vice versa. Perhaps this was the "oneness" he had described. It felt like magic to me, an intimacy of body and spirit that I had never known.

I felt my presence, my entire sense of self, filling with a brilliant white light. *I must be glowing,* I thought. Or did I ask him, "Am I glowing?" I can't remember, but I remember with complete wonder the sensation of being filled with a light. I loved it. My body became a starry explosion from a firework sending glittering sparks in all directions. Like a supernova.

In that moment, I understood the universe.

We met the next day as usual for an espresso near the *palazzo.*

"Today," Antonio started, "I'll teach you the most important lesson."

I noticed the espresso sliding smoothly down my throat. Antonio leaned forward. "Each time you meet someone, whether it be a lover, a friend, a colleague, neighbor or person on the street, find something about them that you can instantly love. It doesn't have to be anything big. It could be their little finger, their laugh, or the way they walk. It can be anything at all so long as you can love it. For me it might be that little dimple I first saw on the side of your smile."

Which, of course, made me grin uncontrollably.

"Whatever it is, if you can find it, and invite love and love's energy into your experience, no matter what you do with that other person, what you create, what you work on, or talk about, share sexually, or engage in professionally, the process will flourish from that initial place. With love you will enhance the outcome of all that you do, no matter what."

We climbed the marble stairs to his *palazzo* penthouse one last time. And there I found much to love.

Grazie mille, Antonio. *Grazie mille.*

STEVE BALDERSON

2

Year of the Whore

After film school, I lived near Manhattan, Kansas, a college town home to Kansas State University. Manhattan has restaurants, bars, and other city-like things to do, but The Little Apple, as they actually call it, is nothing more than a big town or, at best, a teeny, little city.

Unlike the Big Apple, what this speck of a town did not have was a gay bar. Not one. One or two bars were sorta "gay friendly" or had underground in-the-know "gay nights," but there weren't enough gay people to staff a Dairy Queen, never mind keep a business going. A musician friend told me he'd performed in The Little Apple for gay pride, and I laughed and practically gasped. "Gay pride? How many people were there, thirty?"

Over the years, it so happens, the gay population in Manhattan, Kansas, has apparently doubled or tripled or even quadrupled. Local closet doors flew open, college kids who were never in a closet moved to town, and other gay people, unimaginably, relocated there to enjoy the emerging gay scene.

Ten miles outside Manhattan sits Wamego, Kansas, an even smaller town of about 5,000 people. Wamego is the Brooklyn of this Manhattan, suburb-like but far enough away that it isn't truly a suburb. This might sound insane to those of you who live in overcrowded metropolitan areas, but it only takes ten minutes to drive ten miles in Kansas.

Wamego's claim to fame, and quite a claim it is, is the *Oz* Museum, or as I like to call it, the World's Gayest Museum, showcasing the largest collection of *Wizard of Oz* memorabilia on the planet. Why Wamego? The initial collection of memorabilia belonged to a man who grew up and lived in Wamego. I met him once when I was a child and remember stealing one of his Eberhard Faber Design 1 Markers, which, if I sniffed hard enough at the ink, made me think I was getting high.

Oz-related tourism was an economic goldmine for Wamego—being just a short drive from the busy Interstate-70 highway. Every year, hundreds of thousands of *Oz*-devotees gleefully pay homage to the *Oz* Museum. *Oz* fans are a wild, rabid bunch who will part with their money for anything *Oz*-related. Capitalizing on these crowds, Wamego's local barber shop renamed itself the "Scissors of *Oz*." The local Tex-Mex place became "Toto's Tacos." And my sister, of all people, took over the *Oz* Winery near the museum. On occasion, she sold limited-edition bottles of wine to thirsty *Oz* fanatics for $1,000 apiece.

I lived in the residential heart of Wamego in a huge Queen Anne Mansion I called *"Pipistrello."* Think Jefferson's Monticello, except my home was named to honor an endangered brown bat that lived in its rafters before a contractor I hired to renovate the place had killed the poor creature.

Pipistrello (the Italian name for bat) was a turn-of-the century gilded beauty: all original woodworking, stained glass windows, rose brass lighting fixtures, massive ornate wooden doors—all with richly hand-carved detail. When the movie star Karen Black visited, she walked in, took one look around and said, "Now I know why you live in Kansas!" She was right. I loved the place. Of course, she had no idea that my mortgage was only $750 a month.

On the second floor, the mansion was separated in two—each side equipped with its own staircase. The back staircase led to the master bedroom and bath. The front stairs to the guest room and two additional bedrooms. The three bedrooms in the front part of the second floor I converted to film production offices. The editing room was perfectly lit with north-facing windows, I stored all inventory in the equipment and merchandise room, and I took the corner room as my office, home to my computer, desk, and my taxidermy possum named Clarence that I'd asked Santa to bring me when I was four. When a film was in production, you'd find a few employees sprinkled here and there, but on a daily basis I had *Pipistrello* to myself. Peaceful, meditative, and a great place to work and concentrate— I loved this house.

After devouring three chicken enchiladas at Toto's Tacos one day, I returned to my office excited to continue editing my latest film. I was interrupted by the clang of the front doorbell, a sound that echoed through the house. *Who in the hell?* No one ever popped by unannounced. No salesmen. No Jehovah's Witness. No family. No one. At that moment, I happened to be between tasks and had time to kill. On the second clang, now intrigued, I headed to the door.

Before opening it, I peered through the thick beveled glass window in the door's center. A handsome Latino guy, about 5'7," perhaps mid-twenties, stood waiting. I opened the door, "Yes?"

Mr. Latino guy launched into a speech about the magazines he was pedaling. I heard nary a word. His black tee-shirt was pulled tight across well-defined pecs, his pert nipples poking out, and the rest of him just so perfectly proportioned. A gymnast? A wrestler? And big, dark eyes. I loved his eyes. I stared, transfixed, as he confidently assured me I needed not one, but three of his magazines.

Finally, I interrupted him, "I don't really need any magazines."

"Please," he begged. "I really need the money. I need to sell twenty dollars more and after that I'll win. I'll be the top salesperson." He explained how he and his group were from a nearby town, each had picked a street to walk down before heading back to the van. The goal was to be the best salesperson and the winner would get some kind of exciting prize. First, I wondered what the prize could be. What on earth could he want to win so badly?

I realized his story and this situation was all highly unlikely. Everyone knows everyone in the tri-county area and had there been any hot Latino gymnast living nearby I'd have surely known about it. "I'm really sorry, but I just don't need any magazines."

He looked desperate and blurted out, "I just need the twenty dollars... How about a massage?"

I hesitated, giving his body another once-over. There was nothing about this man that spelled gay. He was gorgeous, yes, but a lot of gymnast-wrestler-hunks are straight. Aren't they? Maybe he was a sex worker. Several friends of mine are sex workers and I have nothing against it. I think sex work should be legal, safe, taxed, and with free healthcare. In this case, I wasn't sure he was a sex worker.

"Are you any good?" I asked in a teasing tone pretending to be serious. "There's nothing worse than a bad massage. I get massages every couple of weeks by an incredible massage therapist, so I'm picky."

He looked up at me, sheepishly, "Well, I've only given backrubs to a couple friends, and they say I'm good. And I really need the twenty dollars. Please, sir."

Sir? To hell with *GQ* and *Travel & Leisure*, now this guy had my attention. I still couldn't tell if he was gay, and the whole scene started to feel like a gay porn cliché. But those chocolate brown eyes, those plump lips. Out of nowhere I blurted out, "I don't need a massage but I'm happy to give you a twenty if you'll make out with me for twenty minutes."

"Deal," he said. And walked in.

We barely made it past the foyer before we were locked in a tongue-twisting kiss. He tasted like honey mixed with Red Bull. His soft lips a contrast to his sudden ferocious energy. This quiet little man was all action, his strong arms wrapped around my back, his lips on my neck turned to sharp bites. His hard dick pressed against mine as we mauled each other, madly pulling off each other's clothes.

I had forgotten to shut the front door. As soon as I realized this, I dashed over and bolted the door. We moved deeper inside the house so the neighbors couldn't see.

In one quick movement, he took my pants off, dropped to his knees and wrapped his warm wet mouth around my dick. For a second we held still, and he looked up at me, and winked. *Who winks when they suck dick?* I didn't have time to answer—because he swallowed my dick to the base. One gulp. All the way down. Then back to the tip, another pause, then down again. I gasped, grabbed two handfuls of his thick brown hair, and started fucking his face. He was unphased, a man on a mission, never once coming up for air. I fucked, he swallowed. I fucked harder, he swallowed. Harder again. Three more thrusts, another four, five, fucking his face as hard as I could. So warm and wet and silky. I came in a flash, mashing his face into my crotch, my feet on tip toes, jamming myself as far down his throat as I could get. He wrapped those muscley arms around my thighs, pulling me in even deeper.

He swallowed every drop like any champ gymnast-wrestler would. Over the sound of my own roar and moaning, I could hear him gulping. And gulping. I looked down and saw he'd shot his load, too. How? When? His hands were still around my thighs. No matter, we remained there, in my gorgeous Queen Anne foyer, my dick pulsing in his throat, sun pouring through the beveled glass where—was it just five minutes ago?—I'd first seen him.

I had two thoughts: *My god, this man can suck cock, I think I'm in love.* And, *my god, this man can suck cock, what the hell am I doing?*

I worried that his load—so wonderfully large and thick—might stain the wood floor. I slowly pried my not-yet-soft dick out of his mouth, picked up my tee-shirt and wiped up his cum then wiped my own dripping dick. He looked gorgeous still, kneeling, smiling, but now satisfied and contented.

I pulled up my pants, my dick a large damp mound, and zipped up. He still hadn't moved. To my surprise, I found myself sheepish, tongue-tied. "Um, you know, I gotta say, that was the best head I've had in a long time." I was still dazed.

He said nothing but stood, finally, and faced me, naked. Somehow, he'd even taken off his socks.

"Are you a gymnast?" I asked.

"No, sir," he said quietly, looking up at me as he pulled up his pants. He finished dressing and just as quickly as it started, it was over.

I pulled a twenty from my wallet, handed it to him. He folded it, slowly, carefully, and slid it into a front pocket, drawing my eyes to the bulge in his pants. He said nothing.

I admired his perfect ass as he walked down my front steps. I was about to say goodbye but didn't. Instead, I made note of something I never knew was on my bucket list: "Paid for sex with a total fucking stud. Check."

He turned down the sidewalk and went next door. As I climbed the front staircase back to my office, my mind marveled with questions. *Who was Latino guy, really? How often has he given blowjobs in between selling magazines? He was pretty quick to suggest giving me a massage. Who else has he serviced in the area? Would I ever see him again?* I didn't even know his name.

Even though it was the middle of the afternoon, and I usually work until six o'clock, I decided to turn off my computer and close up my office for the day. I wanted to cherish the oddness and the surprise of what had just happened. And, how, in Wamego, Kansas, it had happened to me.

I went into the kitchen and poured a glass of wine. I took it out to the front porch, which was enormous and screened-in so there would be no bugs. I looked up and down the street, hoping to see Latino guy. I hoped I'd get a glimpse of the van full of all the other gymnasts selling magazines. Maybe I could identify their license plate, figure out which town he lived in, and track him down on social media. Somehow.

Alas, I never saw him again. Not him, nor the van, nor the others.

In the middle of my glass of wine, I decided to open social media and look around. I had received a Facebook message a few hours earlier from a guy named John who graduated Wamego High School, moved to New York City and got a job working at the New York Times.

John was home in Wamego visiting family and wanted to stop by and say hi sometime. I replied, "Sure!" I was instantly excited to visit about what it was like living in The City and was rent truly as astronomical as they say?

I had crossed paths with John when he was barely eighteen years old, and I was in a relationship with the ex. I could tell by the way he looked at me, and flirted, that he was gay. I had no idea whether he was open about it or not. At that time, John applied to work at my graphic design business, but for some reason I can't recall, didn't get the job, so we hadn't had much interaction.

Since the ex's betrayal, it had been on my radar to move out of Kansas. I didn't yet know if I'd end up in Seattle, New York, San Francisco, Los Angeles, or London. I knew I wanted to live in a big diverse multi-cultural city with good food, art, and possibilities for career growth. I became really excited to visit with John about living in The Big Apple. I sent him another reply with my phone number and suggested he come over for happy hour.

I was in the kitchen prepping ingredients for dinner when John texted me, asking if he could stop by.

Ten minutes later I heard the familiar clang of the doorbell, and was soon peering through the beveled glass. With the sun setting behind him, John was all silhouette. I couldn't see his face.

When he stepped into the foyer's bright light, I was awestruck. His transformation from 18-year-old boy to a strapping man of 21 was stellar. Dark blonde hair, pale blue eyes, a chiseled jaw and golden, sun-kissed skin. Even his lips were beautiful, so plump and succulent. Taller than I remembered and now well built, he filled out his navy Polo shirt nicely.

John transfixed me. An unlikely combination of a Ken Doll meets young Marine recruit with a dash of Brad Pitt. The man was radiant.

I mentally undressed him *(...those legs look thick and strong, I wonder what his chest is like? I'm sure his stomach is flat...)* when a voice in my head kicked in: *Keep this platonic. Remember, he's all of 21.* Especially after the romp with magazine man, I'd already scored big that day. *Cool your jets*, the voice said.

So I played polite host, always a safe role, and an easy one. "Would you like some wine?" I asked happily, gesturing toward the kitchen.

"I'd love some," he said, his voice pure silk. *Was he just looking at my crotch? Couldn't be. Okay, platonic, platonic.*

As I poured his wine, I asked him about living in Manhattan—the real one. His ease and self-confidence were pleasing, especially in a man his age. But that beauty, goddamn, I was unprepared for it. Thrown by it. I wanted to just stare at him, so I did the opposite and kept darting my eyes away. I directed a feeling of having love for his confidence and tried to focus my attention there.

"Tell me about Manhattan," I said. I was genuinely interested but also wanted to get him talking so I could watch him unguarded.

"Holy shit, I fucking love it!" he said. "What do you wanna hear? Thai food at 2am. Geeking out like a tourist at the Natural History Museum. How about a gazillion people on every sidewalk. For real, man, I see more humans walking down one block there—every day!—than I saw the entire time I lived here."

His description of living in a city like New York made me immediately jealous and I wished for a moment that I'd never met the ex.

John kept taking, all animation and excitement. Subway station this, nightclub that, something about his job. I wasn't listening. At all. Like a good-host, I set a tray of cheese and crackers on the kitchen island between us. But all I could see were his hairy forearms. His big shoulders. A lovely thick neck. *Did this guy play football in high school? No, more like baseball. Or maybe tennis. Yeah, tennis.*

Don't go there! the voice in my head warned. But what can I say, my dick had other plans. It was buzzing and thickening, all wide-awake again. *This can't be my imagination*, I thought, *the sexual tension is so thick in here I could spread it on one of these crackers.*

I had played tennis in High School and liked it... for about three months. Otherwise, I avoided sports like the plague. The High School principal called me into his office one day and said, "Your life would be better if you quit this art shit and just joined the football team." I made it my mission to be the principal's nemesis each day forward.

Sports weren't as appealing to me as much as the guys who played them. One of my first sexual experiences was with a guy on the High School wrestling team. After we traded blowjobs, the guy, who had a girlfriend, never talked to me again. Perhaps this is where the root of my obsession originates.

I noticed John inching closer every few minutes, gradually moving from his side of the island to mine. Then he was so close to me I could smell him. Fresh and clean with barely a hint of sweat. I wondered if he had a hairy or smooth chest.

He said something about a boyfriend, Bill? Will? Suddenly I was paying attention again.

Are you doing good? That's what I meant to say. But I was dickstracted and couldn't think straight. What came out instead was, "Are you...being...good?"

There was a sly and mischievous twinkle in his eye. "Sometimes," he said, looking straight at me. He held my gaze and sipped his wine, both of us quiet. He tilted his head as if sizing me up. Or making a decision. He grinned, put down his wine glass, and in a move worthy of *Cirque de Soleil,* turned his body closer to mine, leaned onto the island with his elbows while simultaneously dropping his pants and bending at the waist to present his perfectly round ass. It all happened so quick. I looked down. The man wore no underwear. A luscious ass. I stared, marveling at the hair, so much dark blonde hair, between two firm melons. He asked, "You want a taste?"

I didn't even hesitate. I was all instinct. In a flash, I dropped to my knees and stared at those furry muscled cheeks. I jammed my face between them. My tongue darting in and out, circling, salivating, lapping at his hole. I licked him like I couldn't get enough.

John moaned. "I like it rough," he said. "Real rough."

By then I was full-on tongue-fucking him, my hands pulling his cheeks apart, my face wet with my own spit. I ran my goateed chin over his hole, tingling him. John groaned, spreading his feet wider. He pushed back, grinding his ass into me. I pushed, too, burying my face even deeper, chin first, rubbing all the way up and down his crack. Again and again, relentless.

"Yeah, do that," he said, pushing back harder. "Fucking hell, please do that."

I had to grab his thighs to steady myself. I kept at it, grinding, and licking everywhere. Then I leaned down and took one lick—long and slow—from the back of his nuts to the top of his crack. I stopped, catching my breath.

"Your ass," I said, panting, "is so fucking beautiful."

We held still for a minute, both of us breathless. I felt the hard kitchen floor on my knees. I looked around, the room so bright. My kitchen, I thought. I'm on my knees in my kitchen tongue fucking this guy's amazing ass.

I licked my lips and could taste the musk of him. Sweaty and ripe. I closed my eyes, licking my lips, savoring it. I felt high from it all, like I was made for this, for eating a man's butt this way.

"Rough," John said again, this time like a command. I obeyed.

I buried my face back into him in a frenzy of licking, scratching, and biting, slathering my tongue all over him. Both of us moaning. I bent lower and bit his right thigh again and again, practically chewing on him. I squeezed hard on his cheeks, holding him in place. Then I was lapping at him like a dog, big, long licks deep in his crack, as hard as I could.

"Eat me," John said, grinding his ass against me. "Goddamn, fucking eat me."

I did. Relentlessly. For another five minutes. Ten? Who knows. When I stopped, I was panting again. I sat back on my knees and used my sleeve to wipe the spit off my face. Moving slowly, my head spinning, I stood.

Before I could even grip the island to steady myself John was on me, his mouth against mine, suckling my upper lip. Then sliding his tongue in my mouth, lapping at me.

"You taste like my butt," he said. "I fucking love it."

My god, I thought, *he's even hotter than...wait, Latino guy was just a few hours ago! What the fuck?*

John was now stripping in a hurry. He shoved the platter of crackers aside and sprawled himself face down on my kitchen island, his butt positioned just right. I needed no command. I stepped forward, undid my pants, and slid my stiff dick right into of him. To the hilt.

"Holy fuck, you're tight," I said. "And so slippery."

This was more than just my spit. Had he lubed himself before he got here?

I grabbed his hips and jackhammered him as hard as I could.

"I...came...prepared," he said, between grunts. "I...was...hoping."

"I shot a load earlier today," I said, "so no guarantees I'm gonna shoot again."

"Just keep pounding me with that big daddy dick," he said.

Daddy dick? I had never heard the term "daddy dick" before, so this was something new to me. My thoughts strayed into how to categorize him sexually. Would his category be called Dominant Bottom? Bossy Bottom? Aggressive Bottom? There was certainly nothing traditionally submissive about him. Then I wondered, am I in a porn scene? Is this even happening?

It was. His butt was warm and wet and heavenly. That much I knew. I fucked and fucked and fucked in some kind of feverish heat, holding John by the hips, shaking the whole kitchen island. He grunted and groaned, saying, "Yes!" every time I rammed myself in. "Yes, daddy. Yes."

At some point I stepped back and pulled out. I'm not even sure why. I was still rock hard. I looked down and saw semen all over the island. One burst had landed on the cheese and crackers.

"You came? I didn't even know," I said.

John said nothing, but in another masterful maneuver, he spun around lightening quick, dropped to his knees, and took my dick deep in his mouth. Down his throat.

My god, the man has no gag reflex, I thought. *He's so*

fucking perfect!

I fucked his throat hard and rough, like he wanted. I was aware that I was acting the part a little. And since I'm not an actor, it made me a little self-conscious. I wondered if I was being hard and rough enough. The kitchen was filled with wet, squelching, slobbery noises punctuated only by deep grunts and groans. It was all male, all dick and mouth and throat. Then, legs shaking, I shot my load down John's throat.

"Oh my fucking god," I cried out. I'd never felt sensitivity like this, my whole body quivering. I could hear my own shallow breathing. My hands locked around the back of his head.

I have no idea how long I stood like that, how long my dick kept squirting. It seemed like a long time. My eyes were wide open, legs still shaking, as I slid myself out of him. I looked down and, for the second time that day, saw my dick coated with my semen and another man's spit.

I felt a surge of pride for shooting so much. For experimenting being rough with John. For doing two guys in one day—and in my own house.

John licked his lips and stood, a little wobbly. His Brad Pitt Ken Doll hair now a perfect mess. "Where's my wine?" he asked, looking around, bewildered. He smiled, a look so sexy I could hardly take it in. His chin was coated in that same mess of spit and semen. He wiped it off with his hand, then licked his hand clean, sucking each finger.

I pointed to his glass and lit a cigarette, still bracing against the countertop. My legs were steadier but my head was whirling.

John downed his wine, a full glass, in one long chug.

He refilled it and downed it a second time. "Phew!" he said, sliding his pants up. "You're uncut, right?"

Huh? I just stared at him, confused. My dick had just been in his mouth. Right in front of his face. I was a little tongue-tied. "No," I told him. *Why had he asked me that? It made no sense whatsoever. What a bizarre young man.*

He merely said, "I needed that. I mean, damn, I really needed that."

Eventually, we said goodbyes and I showed him out the back door. He was gone.

Usually when making dinner, I listen to an audiobook, a podcast, or some music. That night I decided that silence was the best choice. I had too many thoughts swimming in my mind which needed to be settled and understood somehow.

I contemplated the magic of that day and wondered if there was a gigantic magnetic pull that I'd unleashed somehow. Or perhaps there was a neon sign pointing my way. None of it made any logical sense to me.

After I finished the wine, the *penne arrabbiata* and steamed green beans, I took a nicely scalding shower. Finally, my mind was calm and at ease.

I went into the living room to watch a little something on the television. I was obsessed with the competition cooking show *Iron Chef America*. It was super melodramatic and extremely entertaining.

The deeper into the show I got, the sleepier I got. I wasn't too tipsy because the pasta soaked up most of the wine, but I was very tired.

Suddenly, a knock at the front door. No bell turning. Just a loud knock.

I peered around the corner and switched on the exterior lights. It was a pizza delivery guy. I opened the door, and he told me how much I owed him.

"I didn't order any pizza."

He looked a little dumbfounded and bewildered while searching for his order ticket. He unfolded it and asked, "514 Poplar, right?"

"No," I corrected and pointed, "514 is across the street."

He looked back at me a little embarrassed. "I'm really sorry to bother you."

He had wavy hair with big brown curls, stunning green eyes, with thick and very-kissable lips. "Don't worry about it." I almost hesitated to tell him what was really on my mind, but thought, after this wild day, *fuck it*, and blurted out, "You're really cute."

There wasn't any time to ponder what could've gone wrong because he instantly said, "You are, too."

Off to the races. "What time do you get off work?"

"In an hour, but I have to go home after."

"Maybe stop by tomorrow?"

"Yeah, that'd be cool."

"What's your name?"

"Sean."

"I'm Steve. Have a nice night, Sean."

"Thanks," he stammered and turned to go. "I'll see ya tomorrow."

I slept like a boulder. When I woke up the next morning I felt like a new person. I got out of bed, put clothes on, and walked down the back staircase to make some ginger tea.

As the water boiled, I realized that it was time to turn

the calendar forward to the next month. My wall calendar featured great photographs of Paris. One month was the Eiffel Tower, another might be Notre Dame Cathedral. The month I turned to featured a random corner café with rattan chairs and little round granite tables lining the sidewalk, probably located in the Left Bank. I glanced around the page of dates to find out what celebrations were happening in the month ahead. The full moon. The new moon. Chinese New Year.

Oh, yes, Chinese New Year.

The first thing that popped into my mind was, "Oh my god, it's The Year of the Whore." Yes, somewhere between the Rabbit and Dragon and Ox stands the secret zodiac sign of The Whore. Maybe I'd been born under this secret sign. Surely, I had. I didn't need an astrological chart analysis to tell me so. I was living it.

Suddenly, the wildness of my experiences the day prior made complete sense.

It had been only weeks since I turned forty. Never once was I worried or scared or depressed about turning forty. I know people who fret about it, throw "over the hill" parties and such. But, for me, it was just another birthday. It wasn't until I turned forty that I realized it was magical. I felt like a newborn.

Sean the pizza boy returned that afternoon and our chemistry was unmistakable. Sexually and mentally. He was nineteen. I was forty. So, naturally, we dated for two months. He was beyond bright—sometimes. Had the mind of a forty-year-old—sometimes. Our conversations were engaging and stimulating— sometimes. Having sex with him was good—sometimes. And, alas, he behaved like an irritating teenager—

sometimes.

Reflecting upon the wildness of that day meeting Sean, and earlier John, and the unexpected surprise of Latino guy, I realized the enormous mathematical odds of those things happening. And that they would happen to someone living in Wamego, Kansas, no less. The odds are staggering.

What's even more mind-blowing?

All of that happened and I hadn't even left my house.

STEVE BALDERSON

3
007

A few weeks after I ended it with Sean the pizza boy, I started messaging a guy on The App. I quickly learned he was a Soldier in the US Army and stationed at Fort Riley, a military base just thirty miles from Wamego. Home to soldiers and families of the 1st Infantry Division, approximately 15,000 active-duty service members live at Fort Riley.

The 1st Infantry Division is a combined arms division of the United States Army and is the oldest continuously serving division in the Regular Army (the professional core of the United States Army). It has seen continuous service since its organization in 1917 during World War I. It was officially nicknamed "The Big Red One" (abbreviated "BRO") after the design and color of its shoulder patch.

He looked incredibly muscular in pictures, and he told me he got his strength from being a soldier, not from being in a gym. He had ice-blue eyes, perfectly smooth skin, and sun kissed blonde hair. Probably about six feet tall. Originally from San Diego. There wasn't a thing about this guy that didn't scream STUD.

He was okay sharing cell numbers but for discretion and security reasons, he would not tell me his name. So I nick-named him. "I'll call you '007'," I said. "It just seems to fit."

"I'm good with that," he said.

He was happily married to a woman and had two kids, he told me.

"I'm totally heterosexual except I have this insatiable hunger for sucking dick," he said. "And I mean insatiable."

Hetero? Whatever. A hot soldier with an appetite for dick was plenty good for me.

"Me and my wife have a hot sex life," he said. "But, you know, she can't really satisfy my craving for cock." He was trying to find someone in the area to service and wanted no reciprocation. *A serviceman who needs a man to service? This just keeps getting better*, I thought.

"Every guy I meet wants to suck me, or they want me to fuck them," he said, presenting a problem I refused to see as a problem. But he was clear: that did not appeal to him.

"I'm kind of running out of options," he said. "So...maybe that's where you come in?"

He was lucky. This situation happened to fit my very strict policy of not turning down gorgeous men who beg me for sex.

"Out of the generosity of my heart," I said, and yes, I used those words, "I'd be happy to help you out with that."

After all, he was a soldier and busy defending our

great nation. It was the least I could do.

We settled on an arrangement. It was decided that if I ever wanted to be serviced, no matter the time or day, I could simply text him with the words, "What's up?" Meaning my dick. If he was free to text back right away, he would. Otherwise, I would stop texting. Instead, I was to wait patiently (ha!) until he could reply. Likewise, any time he was hungry and needed "some protein" as he liked to call it, he would text me with, "Need service?" I saved his number in my phone as "007" and he listed me in his as "Sergeant Steve."

About a week later, on a sunny Saturday morning, I was eating breakfast when my phone dinged. It was "007." Suddenly I was wide awake. No coffee needed.

After "Need service?" he wrote, "Free for an hour. Meet me in Sears parking lot?" *To hell with breakfast,* I thought as a I grabbed my keys and hopped in my truck.

My truck back then was a big Dodge RAM 1500 Quad Cab. I'm not particularly macho, but I am six-feet-five and a big truck was one of the few vehicles that I could sit up straight and feel comfortable in.

When I pulled into the Sears parking lot not fifteen minutes later, I noticed his truck entering at the other end of the lot. Suddenly, I was nervous and felt my face flush. I drove to the center of the lot and parked next to one of the random trees scattered around it. This Sears had been abandoned months earlier and the mall it was attached to wasn't yet open, so the place was deserted. I had to admit, 007 was a man with a plan: he'd picked the perfect place for our stealth mission. He parked beside me. Here, the shadows from the tree provided some cover and I could also keep watch in all directions. If anybody drove in, we'd have time to zip up and act like nothing was happening. *No dicksucking going on in this truck.*

He stepped out of his truck and into mine. It was so quiet I could hear my heart thumping against my chest—and was glad he couldn't.

I was happy to see he was even more handsome and sexy than his pictures. Big, blonde, and broad shouldered, he had that all-American, young, military stud look going on. He was not in uniform, and I realized my fantasy had been for this military man to suck me off while decked in his fatigues. Once he was seated beside me—all hot and manly—that fantasy went out the window. I could smell him, a strong scent, all male, something I recognized but couldn't place. Something metallic. Then it hit me. Gunpowder. He's not in fatigues but he reeked of sweat and gunpowder. He was such a manly man I was even more turned on. He turned to me, smiled slyly, and said, "Mornin', Sir," before leaning over to unzip my pants. Within 30 seconds of getting into my truck he had my dick in his mouth and was getting to work. I leaned back, still a little stunned this soldier-stud was in my truck and going down on me. I scanned the lot's two entrances. No cars. Nobody.

I closed my eyes and thought, yeah he's a soldier alright, but goddamn this guy sucks dick like a pro. Whatever the heck he was doing with his tongue and throat and saliva was a wonder, something I'd never felt before. My heart was still pounding, but now because of what he was doing to me. And me trying not to shoot right away. I wanted this to last. He was a powerful man, for sure, and he sucked my dick with an intensity I thoroughly loved. But he was surprisingly tender, too. Wet, but not sloppy. Focused, but gentle. *Did he practice this skill in basic training? No,* I thought, *he perfected it there.*

I know most guys like to be warned when your dam's about to break so they're prepared. Or at least not surprised. When I felt that incredible imminent eruption, and my god I never wanted this to end, I whispered, "I'm getting close."

He gulped even harder, swallowing my dick to the base, his buzz-cut hair scratching inside my thighs.

I shot my first load into him and he swallowed so loud I could hear it. And he kept right on sucking, his head buried in my lap. I kept cumming, shooting, and he kept sucking. I stared at the back of his blonde head in wonder. *How is he even breathing?* No idea, but the man never came up for air. Even when the cum stopped shooting, 007 kept right on sucking.

He slurped and lapped tenderly at my dick until, finally, it began to soften in his mouth. This was my first full-on post orgasm blowjob, and it was amazing. And still, 007 kept his face in my lap, my dick in his mouth. As far as I was concerned, he could suck me like this all day. I even lit a cigarette, blowing smoke out the window in a just-shot-my-load haze—and still he kept at it. *Is there some military slogan about "getting the job done right?"* I wondered. *Because this guy sure was.*

It was heaven.

I finished my smoke and flicked it out onto the concrete—because my cock was getting hard again. I focused on the sensations going through my body. I put my hand on the back of his powerful shoulders and wondered if he'd react. He didn't flinch. He just kept working that wonderful mouth.

After the first orgasm I was in that familiar blissful

state, but as I neared the second I could feel shifts in my body. My leg muscles started to spasm. My neurology was firing on all levels. I broke out in a sweat. I felt my body temperature rise. I imagined this must be what an exorcism feels like. It was wild. For a moment I wasn't sure where we were, or who he was. Or how we got here. Even my vision blurred. But under it all was the wild pleasure of his mouth, his tongue, his throat. All relentlessly working my cock from tip to base and back again. And again. I could even feel my dick getting harder. And somehow harder again.

When I shot my second load, I had what can only be called a full-body orgasm. Waves of pleasure radiated out from my cock and coursed through my entire being. My fingertips, my arms, my chest and hips, down my legs straight to my toes, every inch of me was firing in all directions.

When I landed again, back in my panting body, back in the driver's seat of my truck, I was wiped out. I felt almost weak, like I'd been on some crazy long run that had suddenly stopped. My dick was still on fire, all twitching and hypersensitive, and I had to pull "Double-OMG-7" from my lap.

He raised his head and gave me a big smile. A dazzling smile. "You taste great," he said. "And I mean that. Just great."

"I loved it," I said, my voice hoarse. My mouth dry. "You're talented. And I mean that. Tal-en-ted," I said, drawing out the word. "I can't be the first man to tell you that."

He smiled bright again, sitting up soldier-straight, and looked squarely at me, blue eyes twinkling.

This guy can't find men who want head? I thought.

My God, what's the world coming to?

"I'd love a smoke if you got one," he said.

We sat and smoked. That alone—just watching him sit back, relax, and smoke—was a sight to behold. I stopped staring at him for about ten seconds and thought, *oh fuck who cares, just say it.*

"You're really beautiful, my friend. And that was some outstanding, top-of-the-line, all-star fucking head."

He nodded in agreement, blowing smoke out the window.

"Yes, sir, it was. That all-star cock of yours deserves all-star head. And I mean de-serves it," he said, drawing out the word in a playful imitation.

He took another drag, tipped his head back and blew the smoke out, this time long and slow. I watched as he sat back, closed his eyes, and settled into his seat. "De-serves it," he said quietly. "Yes, sir. It surely does."

I contemplated if 007 was truly married with children or whether he just wasn't out because of the military. The thought of having an affair with a married man didn't offend me at all, nor make me feel badly, but it did bring up some feelings in me that caused me to question the ethics of the situation. So long as both of us were getting what we wanted, it was mutual and ethical.

I always hated the times two days would pass before hearing from him, but I did understand his need for discretion and that he couldn't always explain an impromptu drive to Home Depot.

Although we never met at Home Depot, which was a story he told his wife a couple times, the Sears parking lot was always my favorite place meeting him.

The thing about 007 that was absolute genius, is that

he was so good at what he did that he always brought me to full-body orgasms. This deeper level of experience at the second orgasm was exhilarating. I loved him for it.

It happened every time. His blowjobs were so intense that I could never get to a third round in one sitting. Instead, we'd have a cigarette and talk a bit before starting on Round Three. At the time I thought, you know, even if we weren't doing this, he might be a fun guy to hang out with.

007 was my "service provider" (his term) for several months, until one day, out of the blue it seemed to me, he told me he was being deployed to Afghanistan. He was going off to war.

After our final stealth rendezvous, I saluted him and thanked him for his service.

True to form, he licked his lips. And I never saw him again.

4
No Idea

When writing this book, I looked through my diary and stumbled on a note that read:

1. Damien the Parisian Art Director

2. Jerome the twenty-year-old burlesque dancer attending Cornell

3. Travis1 and Travis2

Who the hell was Jerome the twenty-year-old burlesque dancer attending Cornell? And more importantly who were Travis1 and Travis2? Somewhere in the back of my mind, I imagined Travis1 to be hotter than Travis2, but I had no recollection who these guys were. No idea at all.

I do remember Damien the Parisian Art Director, though.

A few weeks after 007 got deployed, I flew to Paris for a vacation. The first time I went to Paris, I was with the ex, and I wanted to energetically reclaim the city as mine to experience in freedom.

After checking into my hotel on the *Place de la République*, I walked two blocks to meet Damien at his flat along the green and leafy Boulevard Jules-Ferry. The Frenchman, probably around thirty, greeted me warmly at the massive front door. His green eyes immediately took my attention as a sweet smile appeared between his lips. His disheveled coffee-brown hair waved in the air. Damien had a thin, small frame, and I was getting turned on by the idea that I was so much bigger than him.

We climbed the narrow staircase to the third level of his building. His apartment, though quite small, had been well-arranged and clean. His hair more evident as fashionable compared to the tidiness of his home. The view out from his windows was similar to the view from Jimmy Stewart's apartment in Hitchcock's *Rear Window*, which grabbed me. Though it was bright, sunny and in the middle of the afternoon, I noticed there were neither drapes nor blinds on Damien's windows. I wondered how many neighbors watched Damien at night from their flats across the way.

I broke the silence and asked, "What do you do?"

"I'm... Art Director," his soft accented voice seeped into the air.

"Oh cool," I turned to him. "I'm a film director."

He explained as best he could that he didn't speak English very well. All the while, I couldn't help but notice the struggle across his face. I knew enough French to get the gist of what he meant to say.

I figured we didn't need to speak anything other than the "international language," so I walked closer to him and looked down into his gleaming emerald eyes. He said something in French that I didn't understand, feeling the breath of every word, so I interrupted him by leaning toward him for a kiss.

I explored his thin and delicate lips before darting my tongue inside for what I had hoped would be an amazing French kiss. The French invented kissing, didn't they?

Well, turns out, maybe not.

Damien's kissing, if you can call it that, was wet and warm, sure, but the experience, or perhaps his inexperience, reminded me of how it might feel to kiss a fish like the big mouth bass. His mouth hung open in a strange way. He was producing very little movement, just some opening and closing motions. Whatever tongue action he offered for participation seemed pointless. *How was it possible that an actual Frenchman couldn't French kiss?*

His body was thin and lean. I learned that he was what the queer world called a "twink." I unbuttoned his shirt and slid my left hand around his waist to the top of his tailbone. Driven by raw lust, I ran my middle finger at the top of his crack and marveled at how smooth and soft it was.

I slipped my right hand inside his open shirt to feel his smooth and hairless skin. I placed my hand gently on his chest and rubbed him slowly and affectionately. The warmth of his body was soft and inviting. I could feel his heartbeat.

I flicked my thumb over his nipple, hoping to provoke some passion in his lips. Alas, his kiss remained unchanged—wet, open, and motionless. I spread my fingers so that my thumb could remain on one nipple as I reached the other nipple with my pinky.

I focused my attention to the mounds of his ass and

decided to slip my hand even further into his pants, running my middle finger down between his muscular cheeks. When my finger found his hole, a light whimper escaped his open mouth.

His moan made my dick thicken as it pressed against his.

I pressed my finger in circular motions around his hole and then brought it up to my mouth to taste. I used my tongue to wet it and then I returned it to his cheeks, pressing my wet fingertip against his hole so it opened up and welcomed me.

He moaned a little louder and then began to back away.

"Would you... something to drink," he stuttered.

Not at this exact moment, I thought, but instead, I replied, "Sure."

He poured two glasses of wine and handed me one. He then lit a cigarette and offered one to me.

"No thanks," I said. "I've brought my own."

We sat down in small light brown leather chairs and faced each other. He smoked stylishly and leaned back into his seat. In broken English, we discussed design, architecture, and art direction. I told him about my films. After what seemed an eternity, he stood up and walked over to me, and sank down to his knees.

My legs were spread on either side of him, and he looked up at me with both want and need in his eyes. He unbuttoned my pants and slipped his hand inside, wrapping his long thin fingers around my dick. He gently squeezed at it until it got thicker. I scooted a little down in the seat so I could slip my pants down to my ankles. He put his hands on my thighs and leaned in to lick my dick, which was now pointing directly straight up against his face. He licked the bottom side of my shaft starting at the base and ending at the crown.

He looked down at my balls and beamed, *"Zut alors."*

I almost laughed.

His mouth slid over the top of my dick, and he swallowed it down to the base. He demonstrated having no gag reflex as he started swirling his head around in circular motions. His tongue was working magic and I wondered why it didn't do anything while he was kissing me.

His movements were slow and gentle. A building ecstasy was rising inside my body. I grabbed his hair from behind, about to cum any second, but his warm mouth pulled away from my dick.

"Pas encore mon amour," he said. Not yet.

My dick was leaking precum and he lapped at it with his tongue, making long strands as he played around.

This slow and intricate blowjob lasted a really long time; so long, that I began to lose my hard-on. My balls were aching for release, but I didn't understand what was going on. I finally realized that I needed to pee. I asked, "Toilet?"

He pointed to a small door nearby.

I awkwardly got up and pulled my pants up high enough so that I could walk, and I retreated into the bathroom. After peeing, I shook my dick and tried to wake it back up in vain. It was plump and still a little thick but wasn't as bone hard as it was earlier.

I then realized that I was extremely tired. It was a strange position to be in—horny, in need of an orgasm, and yet, simultaneously too tired to really care about having one. Going back to my hotel and having some wine and dinner honestly seemed more appealing than being there. But I decided to give it one last try.

I returned to find Damien still kneeling on the floor in front of the chair, totally naked. Completely hairless and smooth with only a bush of dark brown pubic hair. The sun was beginning to fall toward the horizon and there was a gold and orange light cascading across his body. He looked beautiful. I poured my love into that sight. I stood there for a moment and took in the scene, making mental photographs of everything I could see.

I walked up to him with my dick swinging and stood so that it was directly in front of his face. He started to lap at it again and engulfed me in his mouth. This time he was not so delicate and slow. He was eager. My dick thickened, and even though the feelings of his mouth felt great, I didn't think it was possible for me to get hard again or reach orgasm.

Having had enough, I took a step backwards and zipped up.

I apologized, "I'm really tired."

He wiped his mouth, nodded, and took a sip of wine.

Fatigued, I felt that I could fall asleep at any moment. "*Merci... Merci beaucoup,*" I said, stumbling toward the door. I couldn't think of any other French words to use.

Damien, still naked, walked over to me. He pulled himself up to the tiptoes and kissed me goodbye. Thankfully, it was only a peck.

I pulled my wits about me as I walked out the door and down the staircase to the boulevard.

As I walked back to my hotel, I could feel a sense of embarrassment creeping over my body. Did I lose my erection because I had to pee, or was it that I lost interest in that guy, or was it a sign of erectile dysfunction?

I thought about all the possibilities of each question. I realized that yes, indeed, I did have to pee at that moment and possibly that was the cause. Concurrently, I realized that I wasn't very turned on by thin, twinky guys.

Most of my sexual encounters and lovers had all been masculine and muscular. Short, perhaps, but built like a gymnast or wrestler. I imagine taking a photograph of a normal sized guy with muscles, and then, in Photoshop, just shrinking down the size of the image so that he would be somewhere around 5'4" to 5'6" in height. You'd never know that he was that short unless I stood next to him. Yes, that was my type: short and muscular gymnast wrestlers.

Thin, wispy guys seem too delicate and feminine to me. Even though Damien wasn't feminine acting, *per se*, his facial bone structure did remind me of the *Venus di Milo*, which in turn, reminded me of 90s supermodel Christy Turlington, whom I'd met and gone hiking with a few times. Plus, Damien's delicate frame made me think I could accidentally break him somehow. Like a fine crystal wine glass. Whereas, with short muscular guys, I could imagine picking them up and tossing them around in a fun way without the fear of damage.

Erectile dysfunction wasn't right because I typically have zero issue with that. Maybe it was performance anxiety. If I had to make the choice to sleep or have sex at that moment, I'd pick sleep.

Many years ago, I learned that sexually I am what is considered a top. I had tried bottoming a few times and it just didn't do anything for me. I found it boring and had zero arousal when attempting the activity. But being a total top isn't easy, I found out. Sometimes, you are expected to perform, even when you aren't "up" for it.

For me, if the chemistry isn't right, and there is no sensuality at play, I'm normally not turned on.

Passion turns me on. Knowing someone turns me on. See, desire is something that is built and made. I like the tease, the buildup. Nothing turns me on more than an intellectual conversation followed by a passionate make out session with a short muscular gymnast wrestler. I do get turned on by other types as well, but there needs to be something sensuous and passionate about it. Even if it's just a fleeting encounter.

If you've ever found yourself in similar situations, and left feeling ashamed or embarrassed, let me tell you: there is nothing wrong with you. Total tops don't have to perform "on call" or "by demand." Some people will have sex with anything that moves. Some guys might get an erection when the wind blows. Not me. My dick isn't "on demand" or something that can be ordered like food delivery.

Of course, I didn't know this at the time. When I fell asleep that night in Paris, thoughts swirled around me in self-doubt and shame. *Was I broken? Was there something wrong with me?*

No idea.

5
Relief

I'd travelled to Paris several times over the years and returning to Wamego was always both a total relief and also utterly depressing. I immediately missed the art, the culture, the food and wished I had never left. At the same time, the comforts of returning to my own home beckoned. Thankfully the small regional airport made it possible for me to disembark the plane, climb into my truck, and walk into my house less than thirty minutes later. With daily flights to Chicago and Dallas, I could fly from Kansas to Paris anytime I wanted to.

Jetlagged and slow to wake the next morning, I walked into my bathroom to wash my face. I turned on the hot water knob and leaned over the sink. Nothing but cold water emerged. While I waited for it to warm up, I decided to brush my teeth. In the middle of working in circular strokes on my upper left molars, the water began to warm slightly. A wonderous feeling cascaded over my teeth and gums like a gentle hug. Brushing my teeth in warm water was a new revelation. Never in my first forty years had I ever thought to brush my teeth with warm water. By pure accident, I stumbled upon this remarkable new sensation, and I've never turned back.

I wondered for a moment if my heightened sensory awareness was learned by a combination of Antonio's lessons in Italy, my newfound joy in sexual pleasure and studying Neuro-Linguistic Programming (NLP). NLP is like a combination of neuroscience and psychology. It helps us understand the way the mind works, how it stores memories and emotions, and how we use those stored memories and emotions when we interact with the world.

For the first time in my life, I was beginning to feel that I was actually "in my body." Certainly, I had moments of self-awareness years and years ago, but not until that moment did I truly begin to become consciously aware of the vibrations I experienced. Something as simple as brushing my teeth with warm water—noticing the sensation, really feeling it, loving it, being in the moment consciously—provoked questions about other ways in which I was moving through the world.

Living comfortably from a sensorial level became a new goal. *In what ways could I make sure I was always comfortable?* First, I had to be aware of how I felt in each moment. Moving, sitting at my desk, walking here or there, traveling, sleeping, working, and so on.

Whenever feeling discomfort or unease, I tried to stop and notice the feelings consciously. Starting with a body scan to investigate and find the location of the discomfort and determine where it was coming from, and what might be the cause.

After brushing my teeth, I noticed my skin was itchy. I'd battled eczema, psoriasis, and dry skin most of my life. I had moisturized earlier, but maybe the culprit was the lotion itself. I examined the lotion's ingredients and discovered it was mostly water. Not the cause.

In the mirror, my shirt caught my eye. For years and years my outfit of choice was jeans paired with western style plaid-colored shirts with pearled button snaps up the front. "Snappies," as I called them, were mostly made of polyester. I took off the scratchy shirt to read the label. Indeed, polyester. Why, with a history of eczema and psoriasis, was I wearing material every single day which aggravated it? I had no idea. But at that moment, I decided to only wear shirts made from 100% cotton.

I threw the snappy on top of my bed and went to the closet. I pulled everything out that wasn't 100% cotton and made piles and piles on top of the bed. Two hours later, the closet was mostly empty. I took the snappies to the local thrift shop, and I decided to practice comfort over fashion from that day forward. Remarkably, the eczema and psoriasis disappeared and never returned.

Finding clothing made with actual cotton nowadays is nearly impossible. Most clothing is made from recycled plastic, with strange synthetic blends that feel terrible in comparison. Some of the plant-based materials are decent, but nothing is better for my body than 100% cotton—Pima, Supima, or otherwise.

Later that day, jetlag began to creep in and focusing on work grew pretty problematic. I turned off my computer, closed the office and contemplated the causes of jetlag. Nevermind crossing time zones, there had to be preventative ways to minimize the effects of jetlag.

I broadened my thinking to include my experience of travel in general.

Was there something I could do or change to make the experience easier? I remembered rushing from security to the gate in Paris, worried about making it to the flight in time. *Why was I rushing? Why was I worried?* Another choice might be that I could allow plenty of time and instead of being worried or stressed, I could turn the whole experience into something relaxing and enjoyable.

To help prevent future consequences of jetlag, I decided that from that moment onward, I would plan to overnight at an airport hotel after the long haul, before catching another flight home the next day. Most airplane tickets with connecting flights are still considered part of the same leg of the journey if the connecting flight happens within 24 hours of landing on the previous flight.

Instead of being worried about arriving to the airport on time, I decided to arrive early. Arriving early allowed a leisurely stroll through security, a stop in a lounge or restaurant to have some champagne and a bite to eat. And then leisurely making my way to the gate.

Around this time, I visited Los Angeles and met up with my friend Chef Saad Ghazi, the proprietor of legendary *Canard de Bombay* Indian restaurant.

Saad asked, "What do you eat for breakfast?"

"Some toast," I told him. "Maybe some cereal."

"No, no, no," he advised. "You should be eating a good amount of protein. A grilled chicken breast, or some salmon."

"Grilled chicken? For breakfast?"

"Yes," he smiled. "It's a most excellent choice for your individual body type. You'll see."

The next morning, I took Chef Saad's advice and ate a grilled chicken breast for breakfast. It was an unusual experience psychologically, but a totally amazing experience sensorily. I felt great afterwards and that feeling lasted all day long.

Let me share with you a secret, something I discovered that has completely transformed my relationship with food and my body. It all started when I stumbled upon a book called *Heart of the Mind* by Steve and Connirae Andreas. There was a particular chapter that captivated me called "The Naturally Slender Eating Strategy," which delved into how people mentally process their hunger.

Picture this: you're feeling a bit peckish, and without much thought, you automatically reach for the nearest snack, which more often than not, is junk food. And let's be honest, those who fall into this habit tend to struggle with their weight. Well, my friend, this chapter opened my eyes to the different mindset of naturally slender people.

Instead of mindlessly consuming, these individuals analyze their hunger, questioning if it's genuine hunger or perhaps just thirst. You see, thirst is often mistaken for hunger, and simply having a glass of water can quench that false craving.

But it doesn't stop there. When a naturally slender person decides they are indeed hungry, they carefully consider their food options, taking into account taste and the impact on their body after consuming it.

This strategy resonated with me, and I began to really listen to my body, noting how different foods made me feel. During my NLP training, I discovered that our unconscious minds are far wiser than our conscious minds, guiding us toward what our body truly needs.

There were days when my body craved an entire pepperoni pizza, and I didn't feel guilty about it. Perhaps it needed the sodium and fat that day. But on other occasions, when the pizza didn't feel right, and I ignored that inner wisdom, my body would indeed feel lousy afterward.

I began to notice patterns. Chicken, whole wheat bread, whole wheat pasta, corn, polenta, and fresh green beans made my body feel fantastic, while lettuce, rice, white bread, too much cheese, beef, and shellfish left me feeling uncomfortable and sluggish.

As I continued on this journey, I started to consider each food's nutritional value but never followed any specific diet plan. You see, those one-size-fits-all fad diets don't take individuality into account, nor do they encourage you to ask, "How will my body feel after eating this?"

I embraced the idea of being a Conscious Eater, allowing myself to enjoy what my body truly needed and desired. The outcome? I lost nearly 80 pounds and could finally fit into a size 32" pair of pants for the first time since I was a kid. So, my friend, that's my little secret – it isn't about deprivation or following the latest trend; it's about truly listening to your body and feeding it what it genuinely needs.

When it came to pants, I hated the feeling of wearing a belt. I decided that I would begin to wear only elastic waisted pants. But instead of droopy sweatpants and common lounge pants, I opted to try yoga pants. Some yoga pants are sleekly designed, cut nicely, made from cotton, and when paired with a suit jacket, looked just like suit pants. I also hate the way I feel in tapered pants or skinny jeans, which is the design favorite of the majority on the market. Finding true straight leg or bootcut pants is rare. Finding them in actual cotton is even rarer. If I do come across a pair, I'll buy a size larger and then take them to a tailor to add elastic around the waistline.

Imagine my surprise when, during a routine visit, my doctor celebrated the virtues of smoking cigarettes. Yes, you heard right, a medical professional singing the praises of nicotine. He claimed that nicotine blocks negative synapses from misfiring during moments of high stress, shedding light on why non-smokers often find solace in a cigarette during trying times.

Now, I'm no doctor, but I did find this piece of information intriguing – borderline scandalous, even. Did I bother to fact-check this seemingly outlandish claim? Of course not! There's something to be said for respecting one's doctor, along with dentists, accountants, and attorneys. After all, who am I to question the wisdom of the professionals who've dedicated years of their lives to studying their respective crafts?

So, with a twinkle of mischief in my eye and a cloud of smoke above my head, I pondered the unexpected revelation from my esteemed physician. Just when you thought you knew everything about the hazards of smoking, life throws you a curveball, wrapped in a puff of irony and served with a side of dry wit. Who would've thought?

Sleep has never been an issue for me, but after the great

betrayal by my ex, I'd occasionally be haunted by nightmares where he had moved back in, and we were trying to "work things out." One morning, I woke up in a cold sweat, eyes wide in terror. A swift glance around assured me I was alone, and I heaved a monumental sigh of relief. Thank heavens it was just a nightmare.

As I peered at the clock, I realized 5:32am was no time for any self-respecting person to be up and about. I faced a dilemma: go back to sleep and risk another nightmare or lie there in limbo. That's when it hit me. I decided to create a little practice I'd like to call "The Art of Laying."

There I was, fully committed to the act of laying. I examined the positioning of my arms with the curiosity of a detective, soaking in the experience. But after a few minutes, dissatisfaction crept in. Surely, there had to be a better way to position myself. So, I tried a new arrangement.

Settling into this unfamiliar pose, I scrutinized how each part of my body felt in its new configuration – from my arms to my legs. The verdict? There is no right or wrong way to lay. One moment, a position feels heavenly; the next, it's downright boring. It turns out, there are no rules in the wild world of laying. To truly lay, and I mean really lay, is nothing short of a thrilling adventure.

I decided to take the practice of laying to the streets.

No, not in the way you might be thinking. I mean, while driving. I'll share a story with you:

Once upon a time in a bustling city, there lived a person named Alex. They had discovered the ancient arts of laying and sitting, practices forgotten in the fast-paced modern world. One day, they decided to embark on a journey to spread this newfound wisdom throughout the city.

At first, they practiced the Art of Laying at home, reveling in the comfort and serenity it brought. Then, Alex bravely decided to bring the practice of sitting into the urban jungle. Whenever they found themselves at a red light or behind a leisurely driver, they practiced their newfound skill.

While the city bustled with honking horns and hurried drivers, Alex sat serenely in their car, cultivating the forgotten art. They paid attention to their posture, relaxed their tense shoulders, and gently held the steering wheel, becoming a beacon of calm amidst the chaos.

As the days went by, Alex discovered the transformative power of reframing their everyday experiences. Rather than being annoyed at the erratic driving habits of fellow city dwellers, they wondered about their stories, their fears, and their dreams.

As word spread, people across the city began to embrace these long-lost arts. They practiced laying in their living rooms, sitting in their offices, and remaining calm in the face of irritation. The city's collective blood pressure lowered, people smiled more, and patience bloomed like never before.

It seemed as though Alex had started a movement, a renaissance of mindfulness in the urban jungle. The once-frantic city had transformed into a place where empathy and understanding reigned. By reframing their experiences and sharing their wisdom, Alex brought the power of the ancient arts of laying and sitting back to life, forever changing the city and its inhabitants.

As the tale of Alex continued to reverberate through

the hearts and minds of the people, they embraced another invaluable lesson: the power of self-awareness and the ability to make new choices.

Whenever anyone felt the tendrils of discomfort sneaking in, they were encouraged to investigate the source, to uncover what was at the root of their unease. They learned to seek out solutions, to find the path that would lead them back to comfort and peace.

The citizens of the city remembered that they held the power to change their destinies. The past, with all its decisions and consequences, could not chain them forever. They understood that they could always make a new choice, take a different path, and reshape their lives according to their hearts' desires.

Curiosity became their guiding star, leading them to explore the boundless possibilities of life. With each moment of uncertainty or discomfort, they would remember Alex's teachings and approach the situation with open hearts and inquisitive minds.

And so, the city thrived, its people weaving a tapestry of kindness, empathy, and transformation. They knew that, at any moment, they could choose again, and relief would wash over them like a gentle wave, soothing their souls and reassuring them that they had the power to shape their own destinies.

In the end, the tale of Alex and their teachings of mindfulness and curiosity left an indelible mark upon the world, reminding everyone that even in the face of adversity, they could always find relief by choosing to live with an open heart and a curious mind.

6
The Massage Table

I won the massage therapist Powerball. Famous billionaire Richard Branson's massage therapist, who had also worked at the Ritz-Carlton Half Moon Bay, had relocated to the Wamego area to take care of her ailing mother. For several years, she treated me to some of the most superb bodywork on the planet.

Until she retired.

My search began for a new massage therapist. The next closest town where one could find high quality bodywork was a thirty-minute drive. So, I purchased an Earthlite massage table and convinced the talented therapists I knew to drive all the way to Wamego just to work on *me*. If they didn't need to bring their own table, it would be an easier commute, I figured. I was right. I also bought fresh linens, an indoor fountain, and reorganized my yoga room into a massage room.

The space had an old glass door that, because it had been painted shut from both the inside and outside, never opened. Large windows gave the room a bright and airy feel and the walls were painted baby blue. Big flowing sheer-white drapes covered the windows. The wooden floor was painted bright glossy white, and I installed a thick wall-to-wall plush carpet with added foam underneath for the absolute softest touch to the feet. The room shined with ideal lighting for photography and reading. And, I would soon discover, despite my honest intentions, for sex.

In the supermarket one morning in April, minding my own business, on the hunt for French green beans, I noticed a handsome young guy standing nearby. About 5'8" with a strong, defined muscular body, dark brown hair, stubble on his face, soft blue eyes, baseball cap, and a purple Kansas State University football team sweatshirt. He looked like a cross between a soccer player and a sexy adult Hobbit.

I didn't notice him checking me out until he was standing so close I could see his eyes darting directly to my crotch like a laser. I felt my hips drag me toward him ever so slightly. A magnet of testosterone. I couldn't control the rush of desire building in my veins. I felt my face flush as I smiled and moved along my way, unsure of the protocol in this situation.

A few aisles later, we passed each other again.

He repeated his crotch-gazing and did the slow once-over with his eyes, making sure I could see what he was doing. Not knowing what I should do in such a scenario, I smiled and kept going. Instinctively, I turned and looked back to discover he had a perfectly rounded ass, which was snug in his gym shorts and pulled tight by his slightly hairy muscular legs.

I glanced up to his face and realized he'd caught me

checking him out.

He smiled, a cute mischievous sort of smile.

I had no idea what the hell to say. Not a single word came to mind.

I paid for my groceries and went to the parking lot.

I loaded the bags into the bed of my truck and noticed the soccer-playing Hobbit approaching. God, he was sexy. The small sack of groceries he bought dangled next to the bulge in his shorts. I ran my eyes over his muscular pecs.

"Hey," he said. "I would've come over to say hi at the bar last night, but it was my friend's birthday."

His voice sent a shiver through me. I hid it well. I hadn't been out the night before and wasn't much of a college bar goer. He must have been confusing me with someone else, but I didn't correct him. I wanted to hear more.

"We'll have to hang out some time," he offered.

"What are you doing now?" I asked. I decided to wing it, and pretend that I was, indeed, whomever he thought I was.

"Heading back to my friend's place. They're all still passed out."

"Big party?"

"I'd have invited you."

I smiled but didn't respond.

"But you can come over now if you want to," he said.

For some reason I can't understand, I was soon following him as we drove out of the grocery store parking lot. It was like being in a trance. Less than a mile away we pulled up in front of a small ranch-style beige house and I parked at the curb.

I got out and walked up to him. His purple sweatshirt

pulled tight across his brawny pecs; his brown hair slightly disheveled, begging me to yank it. He had a daring look but said nothing. He just led me inside.

It was pin drop silent. I saw zero evidence that any roommates or friends were awake. Probably still passed out, like he'd said.

No doubt there'd been a party the night before. Piles of ratty cigarette butts stuffed into overflowing ashtrays, empty beer bottles and cans strewn about, several half-finished bags of chips and candy, a greasy ripped-up pizza box—in short, everything a props-person might dress the set with if you were about to film a scene at a frat party.

He walked quietly, and I followed him into the kitchen, watching his ass with every step. I felt my cheeks flush. His bicep flexed as he removed some yogurt from the sack and put it in the fridge. He turned to me and whispered, "Follow me."

We tip-toed down the staircase to a brightly lit basement. A girl was passed out on a puffy olive-colored sofa and another body lay covered by a plaid blanket. Hard to tell if it was male or female. No one stirred. The smell of stale beer overwhelmed me.

What the hell was I doing here?

He led me into a bedroom and slowly, silently, closed the door. Not even a click as it shut. A girl had clearly decorated this room. Pink walls, pink throw pillows, stuffed animals of all sorts, and a pink comforter with hearts on it.

"Is this your room?" I whispered.

"What?" his face grimaced. "No, it's my friend's."

"It's... pretty," I said.

"Shut up," he laughed, turned to me and leaned up to

kiss me. No thought. No plan. Just passion and the weight of him pressed tightly against my body. His mouth and lips were warm and strong. He tasted raw, like animal sweat and desire.

I ran my hands down every inch of his tight muscular body until they landed on his perfectly hard, Olympian ass with its smooth, soft skin. This guy was a total jock. Definitely soccer. Nothing about his appearance suggested he was gay. Not one clue. But here we were, wrapped in each other's arms.

"I wanted your dick the moment I saw you," he said, slipping his hand down my pants, wrapping it around my rock-hard cock.

My hand snaked into his shorts and found his warm, muscular crevice. My middle finger found his tight hole, and I pressed against it.

He moaned and whispered, "Not here."

He dropped to his knees and undid my zipper. When he took out my dick, a pained moan of desire escaped his lips. He didn't waste any time filling his mouth. The warmth of his tongue slid up and down, up and down, and he looked up into my eyes.

Suddenly, we heard a door open and shut in the hallway. He froze. Someone had gotten up to use the bathroom.

"Shh," he said, standing up.

"What is it?"

He kissed me hard, like we might never kiss again.

"Let's go," he said.

He fled the room. I stuffed my hard, saliva-covered dick into my pants, positioning it to the left so it fit, and I put my hand into my pocket to disguise the bulge. I followed him up the stairs into the kitchen, watching his ass flex with each step.

"Where's your room?" I asked.

"I don't live here," he said. "I'm from Kansas City, just here visiting my friends for a few days."

"Damn," I said.

"Yeah," he agreed and looked at me desperately.

He went to the sink to get a drink of water. His completely round ass was so perfectly round it didn't look real. I wondered if each cheek was the exact size for each of my hands to spread out and grab. I couldn't resist. I walked up and checked. He moaned even deeper this time.

"I need it," he groaned.

"I know."

Sure enough, his ass fit perfectly into my hands.

"I'm already precumming," he whispered, bending his hips over the sink. "I want you inside me so fucking bad."

We were seconds from being caught. My dick was still hard from his wet mouth, and I decided, *fuck it*. "Follow me to my place."

"I can't. That wasn't my car."

"Then come with me and I'll bring you back."

He stared into my eyes for a full ten seconds. He was so handsome, so horny and beautiful and honest. I could see the desire and fear.

"You can trust me," I whispered.

He led the way, and we were out the door, in my truck, driving the fifteen miles toward my house in the next town. I felt his eyes on me. The sexual tension nearly made me shake. In the passenger seat, he slid his hands to his crotch and slowly rubbed the outline of his dick.

What the hell was I doing? Here I was, driving a

stranger to my house so that I could fuck him and then drive him back to his friend's place. It would make more sense if both houses were in the same city. But it was Kansas, and never in my life had a totally hot frat boy muscle jock soccer-playing Hobbit wanted me to fuck him. I figured this might be my only chance.

I realized I didn't even know his name.

"Gus," he told me.

We parked and I took the groceries inside, thankful that I had only bought vegetables and nothing had spoiled. He stared at the bulge in my pants and walked up to me. As I shut the refrigerator door, he slid his hand in my pants and grabbed my dick, sending shivers through my entire body. My dick started throbbing in his strong hand. He grinned and moved his body closer to mine. Heat radiated from his strong chest.

There was nothing more to say so we started making out. His tongue darted around mine, our lips locked together. He tasted salty and sweet.

I reached my arms around him and picked him up. He was solid muscle, not as light as I had expected him to be. I struggled but carried him to the massage room and dropped that perfectly round ass right on top of the massage table, so our faces were more at the same height.

"Is this where you bring all the boys?" he asked.

The foreplay was intense. Biting, licking, wrestling our arms around each other. He wrapped his beefy legs around me and pulled me closer, ramming me into him. We kissed like wild animals.

He scooted off the table and slipped his shorts down, propping one of his legs on top of the massage table. His perfectly positioned hole was visible and seemed to wink at me. I admired his solid muscular legs and that broad, powerful back. I ran a hand down his spine, gently, carefully, using each of my five fingers to caress the contours of his muscles. He was perfect. He grabbed my hand and slid my fingers over his tight, eager hole.

"Give me that big thick daddy dick," he begged.

Again, with the daddy dick. This must be some kind of slang popular with the twenty-year-olds. Not that it mattered. I didn't need to research it, nor did I need to understand it, to know I was about to give him what he wanted.

I bent down and eagerly dove my face into the mounds of solid muscle. I plunged my tongue in and out of his hole, getting it wet and ready with my spit. He constantly whimpered and moaned, causing my dick to throb harder with anticipation.

I tongue fucked him until his hole was thoroughly wet with my saliva. I stood up and positioned my dick against his slick pink hole. With a little shove, my dick slid into him easily.

"AAAHHHH," he cried.

More and more of my dick disappeared inside his hole.

"Uhhh fuck!"

Entering him was an extraordinary raw pleasure— warm, tight, total. I'd never felt such pleasure as his hole swallowed my cock and my hips felt the heat of his rounded ass. He smelled like a mix of marijuana and peppermint toothpaste. Utterly fresh.

I grabbed his hips firmly. My dick twitched inside Gus's ass. I moved in and out of him slowly but steadily at first, wanting to savor each sensation—warm and soft, firm and wet.

"Yes," he groaned, "fuck, yes."

I was silent and focused, determined to share this pleasure with him.

"Yah, right there," he moaned.

Gus taught me how to understand how another man's body works, and where to position my dick so that it would graze against or hit his prostate. Each ass is different, and sometimes, the angle or the positioning matters.

With Gus, I liked exploring his ass to find out how to best please him. And for whatever reason, the way his ass was built fit my cock like a puzzle.

I increased the rhythm of my thrusts into him, reaching my left hand down to brace myself on the massage table to keep balance. My right hand found his muscular chest, slid across his hard pec, and flicked and twisted one of his stiff nipples.

"Fuck," he growled.

I grabbed his hips and thrust into him harder, deeper. His hole gripped my dick tighter. I looked down and watched my dick sliding into him, pulling back out, and thrusting into him again.

"Oh fuck," he moaned. "Fuck yeah, give it to me!"

My balls slapped against him with each thrust.

"Oh fuck!" he whined.

The warmth of his ass felt so fucking great I knew I couldn't hold off much longer. I felt the inevitable.

"I'm... getting... close," I grunted.

"Fuck yes," he cried, "give me that load."

"Yeah," I pounded him harder, "you want it?"

"Fuck yeah," he grumbled, "breed me with that big daddy dick!"

He pushed himself backwards into me, bouncing on my dick, driving it even deeper.

Smack! Smack! Smack!

"Fuuuuck!"

I rammed into him, my dick erupting in spurts. I stayed as far inside him as I could, filling him with cum.

"AAAHHHH!" he cried.

His ass twitched, and his hole squeezed my dick as his orgasm fired across the massage table. Each shot of cum firing made his hole twitch around my dick. My whole body trembled. After a few spurts, he was empty, and his ass began to relax its grip. I stayed inside him until I caught my breath and slowly slid out of his tight wet hole.

"Fuck that was good," he groaned.

Relaxed from head to toe, and completely satisfied, he lay down on the massage table. I climbed on top of him, embracing him. He turned to kiss me; his eyes filled with pure ecstasy.

On the drive back, we learned more about each other. He attended college, wanted to get into healthcare, and become a nurse practitioner.

"How often do you come to the area," I asked.

"Every couple months."

"You should let me know next time you're coming."

"Fuck yeah, I will."

"Do your friends know you're into guys?"

"One does," he said. "She's cool though. We keep it on the DL."

"What's DL?"

"Down low. Between us."

"I see."

We pulled onto the street where his friend's house

was.

"Stop here," he said, "that way I can just walk up and say I was out for a jog or something."

I stopped my truck.

His puppy dog eyes looked over to me and he said, "I need your big dick again."

"What a coincidence," I said sarcastically, "it needs your ass again."

We exchanged numbers and made plans to check in with each other the next morning.

On the drive back I contemplated how amazing it was to have sex in a sunny, bright room. The sight of watching my own dick thrusting in and out of Gus's exquisite ass replayed in my mind. The lighting in that room was exceptional, inspiring me to prefer sex during the daytime, with the lights on and the shades up. I wondered: *are the people who have sex at night, in the dark, in secret, ashamed? Do they feel guilty about having sex?*

I texted Gus at eight o'clock the next morning and arranged to pick him up near the place I had dropped him off, down the street from his friend's house.

Fifteen minutes later, he was bent over my massage table, and my dick was sliding into that perfectly round ass again. Each time with him was more phenomenal than the last. Was it the light of the room? The way his firm muscular body got me hard in seconds? Was it some magic of the massage table? Who knows.

I bought the massage table for genuine massage therapy. Such a joy to discover with Gus, it was the perfect height for a different type of body work. Truly one of the best purchases I've ever made.

STEVE BALDERSON

7

The Porn Star

Summertime came and I decided to begin working on a screenplay loosely based on my experiences in Italy with Antonio. One of the first questions I faced was how to cast it. When John Cameron Mitchell directed *Shortbus*, he cast the film even before the script was finished. Because that film required consensual sex between adults, Mitchell included the actors in the process. As in, who would feel comfortable having sex with whom, and what was each actor willing or not-so-willing to do.

My friend Peter Stickles, who was in *Shortbus*, called it "a magical experience." With this new film, my intention is to capture the feelings I had discovering the ex's betrayal, how I fled to Venice to heal, and to also recreate, in explicit detail, the sexual reawakening I experienced with Antonio. To make an artistic and cinematic feature film that happens to include explicit sex scenes.

When casting a film that includes explicit sex, one

approach is to cast professional actors who are willing to "perform" explicit on-camera sex. Another approach is to cast porn stars who happen to be good actors. I could see pros and cons of both.

Porn stars, I'm sorry to say, are known to be terrible actors. That's okay, since no one watches porn expecting Oscar-worthy acting. But I've watched some perfect comedic timing and heartfelt acting that genuinely moved me—in porn films. The bonus with porn stars is they're usually beautiful and unabashed about being naked and having sex on camera, with entire film crews on set and watching.

Professional actors are, as a group, generally less comfortable baring it all on screen, let alone actually having sex. Even if they agree to it, my fear is that when the time comes to actually shoot the sex scenes, they'd insist on a body-double or flat out refuse to do the scene as scripted.

You see my dilemma.

To resolve this, I reached out to several porn stars I also thought were talented actors. One young guy, early 20s, blonde, was built like—*oh, what do you think*—a 5'5" gymnast wrestler. But in his case, the Olympic version. I'll call him Joe, which is neither his porn name nor his real name.

Though his training and background was mostly stage-based, I was pleased to learn he'd studied acting. Even fully dressed, the camera loved him. And as an actor, he was a natural.

Joe and I spoke on Facetime to discuss the project and how we'd find potential screen partners for him. By the time we met in person, I felt like we really knew each other.

Three weeks after our first conversation, I flew halfway across the country for that initial meeting and invited him to join me and a screenwriter friend for dinner. The first time I saw Joe in person, I gasped. He was way more handsome than he appeared on film, which I attribute to poor cinematography, like over-lighting and flat camera placement. In natural light, this guy was gorgeous.

Over dinner, I focused on getting to know Joe beyond his beauty, as a three-dimensional person. After my screenwriter-friend left, Joe and I were alone—and on our fourth glass of wine.

"Did you ever have to do a sex-scene with someone you weren't attracted to?" I asked.

"Oh yeah, all the time," he said. He told me a hilarious story of getting fucked by a guy on film that, he said, looked like a lifeless drill sergeant wearing an oversized uniform. "I wasn't the least bit turned on by him," Joe said. "He wasn't my type at all. But you, I mean, a guy like you, that's my ideal type." He looked directly at me, slowly nodding his head.

Ignoring the immediate stir in my crotch, I thought: *Wow, how did I not notice this kid's beautiful eyes?*

"Awesome," is all I said. I made a mental note: in the future learn how to say exactly what's on my mind. I knew I was just staring at him, but I couldn't help myself. A cleft chin. Thick wavy blonde hair. Lips that I wanted to...

"Do you want to go somewhere and have another drink?" he asked, startling me out of my trance.

"Absolutely," I said.

"In public or maybe somewhere," and here he paused, "well, just more private?"

"Both," I said. "I'm up for just about anything." Oh fuck, I thought, I hope I don't sound desperate. I didn't feel desperate. Just flattered. And eager.

Joe smiled. "I know just the place."

We taxied across town to a popular gay bar. A quiet place that night, the crowd sparse. We ordered wine and sat on the outdoor patio so we could smoke, talk, drink. Joe is smart, creative, and articulate.

I asked Joe more about his life off camera, off stage. What I learned surprised me. He had a culinary degree from *Le Cordon Bleu*, dreamt of opening a bakery, and currently had two paintings in a show in Brooklyn.

I know there's always more to a person than we can know when first meeting. I was even more taken with him. The man was proving even more impressive off-camera than on.

Then out of nowhere he said, "Should we have sex before working together?"

Mid-sip, I nearly choked. I thought about it, flashing on a story my film-school mentor, Eric Sherman, had told me. On the spot, I told Joe the story, as I remembered Eric telling it to me.

"My father," Eric said, "was among the last of Hollywood's Golden Age directors. One day, he came home from directing at one of the big studios. My mother asked him, 'How'd it go on set today?' 'Excellent,' my father said, 'I slept with Bette Davis.'"

Eric paused. "What do you think my mother said?"

"I have no idea," I said, "but I can't wait to hear."

"She sat down at the kitchen table," Eric told me. "She leaned in toward my father and asked, 'So how was it?' And they proceeded to talk about all the details. And

I mean every detail!"

At that point in my life the story was an eye-opener. Just the idea of having a sexually open relationship with someone—where love and sex didn't have to go hand in hand—blew my mind.

I also recalled in class one day that Eric said film directors should avoid having sex with their actors during filming. "It's best to wait until the film is completed," he told our class. But his father had started an affair with Bette Davis in the middle of production. Later, when Eric's father wanted to end the affair, Bette started ignoring him on set and off—and would not follow his direction. "The rest of filming—a trainwreck," Eric said. And in the film, knowing this, you can actually see the moment Bette Davis had stopped listening to her director. You can see the change on film.

"So," I said, "I'm thinking if we sleep together *before* collaborating the energy between us won't change. If we were in the middle of filming something together, I'd say let's wait until the end, and then, you know, I'd tear your clothes off. Either before or after. But not in the middle."

Joe smiled again. "Great!"

After a nice talk and some smokes, we returned to the bar inside. Within the space of thirty minutes the place was packed.

As we walked through the crowd, I noticed almost everyone recognized Joe. I felt a little awkward being with him, wondering if everyone was sizing me up, wondering why this Adonis was with me of all people.

Joe saw a drag queen friend of his, and turned to me, "Let's talk to her, she's amazing. I'll introduce you!"

After shaking hands, the drag queen and Joe talked

about her upcoming shows. Joe told her he used to go-go dance at the same bar. The drag queen asked if Joe was still with the famous porn studio, and I overheard him say something to the effect that his relationship with them "fell through."

Joe whispered something to the drag queen, and she replied, "I'd heard the rumors. Good that you're out of that situation."

After some more chit-chat, Joe noticed the owner of the bar had arrived. He took my hand and led me over.

He introduced me to the owner, a friendly fellow about seventy with a nice grin and robust personality. As he and Joe got caught up, I looked up and noticed a nearly naked go-go dancer, dancing on top of the bar mere feet away. He was Latino, totally smooth skin, lean and perfectly muscular. A body of a dancer, not a weightlifter. He wore a cobalt blue jockstrap, a matching leather harness across his chest, sneakers, and nothing else. The go-go dancer smiled at me. I was a little afraid to look at him for too long, so I admired his form and then returned to the conversation Joe and I were having with the owner.

A little while later, Joe took some one-dollar bills from his pocket and handed me a couple. "For tipping the dancer," he said.

The go-go dancer lowered himself, bending elegantly, so he was closer to us. Joe reached up and flirtatiously stuffed a dollar into the waistband of the guy's jockstrap. The dancer smiled in thanks.

Joe and the go-go dancer talked about both being in porn, what shoots were on the horizon, and with which co-stars.

While they spoke, I took one of my singles and hooked

it into the waist of his jockstrap, making sure my middle finger extended down to the top of his crack.

The go-go dancer turned his attention to me. He danced a little more, staring directly into my eyes. I hooked the other dollar into the strap that hugged his left butt cheek. He leaned over and kissed me. He tasted like honey. His tongue was soft, and the touch of his lips passionate and tender. He pulled away and moved his mouth closer to my ear and asked me, "Are you in porn, too?"

Dumbfounded and a little shocked, I thought, *really? Really, me—average me?* To be fair, it was cold, and I was wearing a down jacket, so he had no idea that I wasn't buff underneath. So, I lied through my teeth and replied, "Yes."

He smiled and said, "I'd like to see them," and dove in for another kiss. I couldn't believe it. Here I was, an average guy in a crowded bar full of hot guys and the sizzling go-go dancer was into *me*. Part of me felt like I was being tricked or perhaps the butt of a joke, and the other part of me was savoring the soft taste of the go-go dancer's lips. So, I stopped thinking about the possibility of being part of a joke.

While the go-go dancer and I were making out, I reached my hands up to his muscular thighs, and slid my hand underneath, in between them, across his dick and balls, to the place where his jockstrap pouch stopped, and his ass began. I glided my finger up to his hole and teased it. He kissed me harder.

"Give me your phone," the go-go dancer said.

I did, and he typed in his number and sent himself a text message.

"There's my number. Text me tomorrow."

He kissed me again and I felt the smoothness of his warm skin. I gripped his biceps, those big thick smooth bulges, I could feel his sheer musculature, his strength.

Joe smiled at me and said, "He likes you."

I felt like I was living in an alternate universe.

The owner bought Joe and I another round of drinks. Every now and then I'd look up to the go-go dancer who continued to smile at me.

I moved closer to kiss the go-go dancer. He leaned down. We kissed again. A soft, tender kiss. I couldn't believe this was happening to me. Then, in a graceful move, he twisted around so his ass was in my face, and I darted my tongue right into it. I focused on the sensation and wildness of the moment, totally unaware of the crowd of men standing nearby. I kept my tongue-fucking brief. Just long enough for him to return to kissing me and say, "I want you in me tomorrow."

"Okay, baby," I said and kissed him again.

I returned my attention to Joe, who scooted closer to me so that his back was pressed against my stomach. Instinctively, I reached down and hooked my arm around him. He pressed back, grinding into me.

After another round of drinks, we were outside. We walked to the corner and shared a cigarette and began making out madly on the sidewalk. My dick was bulging out of my jeans, and he was grabbing at it. I reached around to feel his perfect ass, so incredibly tight and inviting. We slid down the wall to the side of the building away from the curb and I stuck my hand into the back of his pants and darted down toward his hole.

When my finger found it, and I began stroking him, he made the most delicious sounding moans and whimpers, barely audible and oh-so-hot. I could feel my dick throbbing. I didn't care that we were on the sidewalk. I didn't care who could see. All I cared about was this insane moment, this insane evening, Joe's insanely sexy ass. And how I felt at that moment like the luckiest guy in the world.

The next morning, I woke up to find Joe naked, his back spooned up against me, still sound asleep. He looked like an angel. A studly gorgeous one, but still—an angel. I pressed my raging hard dick between his ass cheeks. He was suddenly grinding into me, apparently not the sleeping angel I'd seen just moments before. I kissed the back of his head and slid my hand down the right side of his body. So warm, and all muscle. I gripped his hips and pulled him back into me. Then I started grinding into him so that my dick slipped down his crack and toward his balls.

He moaned and whimpered quietly again. *Good god, what a sound. How could anyone resist it?*

He turned his head back and I leaned over to kiss him. We kissed tenderly, then wildly, my stiff dick sliding up and down his crack.

I reached for the lube on the nightstand, greased up my fingers and spread it onto his hole. Then slid my dick inside—but just a little. Teasing him. Teasing both of us. His moans got louder, and made my dick get even harder and I slid deeper inside. Each thrust slow and deliberate. I wanted to savor this, my dick inside this beautiful man, both of us moaning in pleasure.

"Focus your attention on everything you see," I told him, my dick buried to the hilt. "Name each thing in your head. The blue wall. The glass of water on the bedside. The square patch of sun on the floor. One thing at a time.

Do it Joe," I whispered in his ear. "Do it for me."

For the next few minutes, I slid in and out of him, so slow. He moaned out loud, so loud, when I was all the way back in. His ass gripping me, pulling me in.

"After you fill your head with all that you can see, shift your attention to everything you hear. Every. Little. Sound," I said, thrusting into him with each word. "Listen to the sounds you make... the ones... I make."

His moaning was making me crazy. I started fucking him hard, banging in and out. "And once you've heard as much as you can hear, focus on everything you can feel." I thrust into him again. "How do I feel inside you? Can you feel the thickness, my dick all the way inside you?"

"It's... it's... oh, fuck, don't stop. It's just so good. So good," he said, whimpering and moaning as he spoke.

"Describe it to me," I said and stopped thrusting, my dick deep inside. "Tell me. Right now, how does it feel?"

"I feel your dick throbbing... and I can feel the warmth," he said. He sounded on the verge of tears, that mixture of pleasure, vulnerability, and lust.

"I feel your ass gripping my dick," I whispered. "Like it wants me to stay there." I thrust into him again. "You feel that, you're gripping me." Another thrust, and another, each followed by his sweet moan.

I moved my hand to his leg and lifted it slightly. Keeping my dick deep inside him, I rolled him onto his side. I kept sliding in, moving slowly back out, savoring his tight grip on my dick.

"I could stay like this all day," I said, "just buried inside you."

"Same," he whispered. "I haven't been fucked in this position before. It's amazing."

I held him in a soft embrace for another few moments, gently kissing the back of his neck. I started moving my dick again and flicked his nipples.

"Are they sensitive?"

"Sometimes," he said, "but not usually. Right now they're kinda on fire."

His hands held onto the arm I'd wrapped around his torso.

I slowly slid out of him, got out of bed and rolled him onto his back. I grabbed him by the hips and pulled him to the edge of the bed. I lined up my dick to his hole and thrust into him again. Now I could look into his eyes. See the look on his handsome face change as my dick slid all the way in.

I bent down to kiss him.

"Give me your tongue," I said. I sucked it into my mouth and pulled on it with my lips, gently biting him.

He moaned and I released it.

"How was that?" I asked.

"Do it again. Please just do it again."

We kissed wildly, passionately, animalistic even. His hard dick, so large for his small frame, throbbed against his abs, thick precum oozing onto his taut belly.

I felt myself getting close. It was time. I pounded into him relentlessly, pulling at his hips, holding him in place. His eyebrows raised in wonderment, then he closed his eyes, his head lolling to one side.

His moans were a trademark, just so damn sexy, and hearing them now made me erupt. I blasted inside him, could feel the semen shooting out, volley after volley, unloading into him. It felt like I'd filled him with my cum.

I stayed inside, pulsating. Joe was jerking off, stroking faster and faster.

"Do you want me inside when you shoot," I asked.

"Please don't move," he begged. "Keep that thing inside me. Deep...so deep."

I could tell by the way his ass was beginning to grip my dick even tighter—the tell-tale sign of a bottom about to shoot his load—that he was getting close.

A moment later he let out a great moan and it happened, his cum shooting in big ropes up to his chest, his neck, his chin, even onto the sheets. He came and came and came, and I held him close, kissing him, my dick (to my amazement) stiff as a board again.

We stayed there, me standing at the edge of the bed with my hardon inside him, and Joe on his back catching his breath. "Aren't you just the little cum machine," I said, my voice a whisper and all affection. He smiled, wiping semen off his chin with his fingers and holding them to me like an offering. I sucked his fingers clean, gladly, and found myself moaning as I savored the saltiness of him.

I let my dick deflate, well, mostly deflate, before sliding out of him. I climbed back into bed beside him.

"Come here baby," I said, tugging him by the shoulders, inching him toward me. "I could do this with you all day long."

We held each other close and kissed softly, his mouth and tongue warm and soft, and tasting of cum. He must have shot some into his mouth. That thought—and the taste of him—got me stiff again.

"All day?" he asked, with a devilish grin.

I stared into his handsome face, his blue eyes bright, his blonde hair a sexy disheveled mess. "Oh, all day," I said between kisses. "And into tomorrow, too."

We held each other and snuggled close. I could feel

his cum-soaked chest and belly against me, our wet dicks mashing together. He smelled so manly, all sweat and semen and the wonderful reek of sex. All so entirely male.

"You're comfortable," I said quietly, my voice a confession. "I mean, you're really comfortable."

"So are you," he said, holding me tight, his face pressed against my chest.

STEVE BALDERSON

8

The Birds & The Trees

Contrary to what nearly all churches, governments, institutions, and religious fanatics will tell us—there is no such thing as pornography.

According to Merriam-Webster: "Pornography refers to a visual or written work designed to cause sexual arousal."

That is where the word immediately becomes ambiguous. What causes arousal? Something which is erotic, maybe. Is that always the case? Not at all. We've all seen erotica which isn't arousing. I'm not turned on by heterosexual erotica, for example. I'm able to admire the beauty of the bodies, or the photography, but it stirs nothing sexual in me. So, is it safe to say that art considered erotica is not pornographic?

It gets trickier by the sentence. Art accepted in one culture as religious might be considered erotica in another. Both of which might be considered pornographic and banned by another.

Director Bruce LaBruce told me on the *Filmmaking Confidential* podcast, aside from the Vatican having the largest collection of gay erotica on the planet, the word pornography has evolved into a description of something we might simply be obsessed with, such as "food porn," "travel porn," and so on. Some of which might arouse our imagination, certainly. To stimulate our senses. But sexually? Probably not.

We need a new word.

Years ago, I made a documentary called *Phone Sex*. I invited everyone in my address book: celebrities, family, friends and even the local house painter, to call my voicemail and answer the question, "What is sexy?"

I was amazed to discover that no two people said the same thing twice.

Pop star Josie Cotton replied, "Sexy is probably a biochemical reaction in the brain. I would say, in terms of feeling, it's something to do with the suggestion of the euphoria one experiences in sex. Now, that's very literal, but the suggestion of sex is always more sexy than actual sex? Maybe not. But that's a possibility."

Comedian Margaret Cho told me, "I think what's sexy is a kind of unconsciousness about what's sexy about yourself and allowing yourself just to fully be in your body and in the moment, and in the reality of who you are and what you're doing."

Porn star Ron Jeremy thought, "To me, sexy is in the eyes and the mind of the beholder. For every gorgeous guy and girl you see, there's somebody out there who's tired of having sex with them. Sexy is very cerebral and very personal. It usually also implies 'attractive to look at and in shape.' But then again, a person could find (the opposite) sexy. It's an internal, cerebral thing. If one person finds another person sexy, then they are sexy. You can be sexy if one person finds you that way."

Nothing sexually described or expressed causes sexual arousal in everybody. One person can be aroused by something which can be a total turn-off for someone else. Not everyone shares the same reaction to the thing they're observing.

What I might describe as beautiful, someone else might define as ugly. For every person who enjoys the color orange, there's someone else who can't stand it. How can this be? If the very same thing can be both things to different people, which idea is true?

Neither.

The truth is simply what IS. There is no judgement in what IS. It just is what it is. Like a tree.

There is no such thing as a good tree or a bad tree. Similarly, there's no such thing as an erotic, explicitly stimulating tree. Is there? I suppose it's possible that certain birds get turned on by towering, big, thick trees. Maybe so. If that's the case I'm sure there are other birds who prefer to nest in lighter, graceful, delicate trees. Neither is good or bad or right or wrong. A tree is a tree, and a bird is a bird.

Let's examine this scenario. Two birds are having sex on a branch, and another bird lands across the way in search of food. The bird looking for food does not, likely, see the fornicating birds and think, "Oh my God, how nasty, how dare they, the obscenity!"

Thanks to the Church, our species has been denied any aspect of truth or realness as it relates to the human body ever since the Middle Ages. We've been told throughout millennia to be ashamed of looking at a naked body. Let alone the pleasure of being a naked body ourselves.

The fear of sexuality remains as ridiculous today as it did in the Middle Ages.

Like the birds and the trees, a portrayal of our species' sexuality is simply a portrayal of our species' sexuality. Whether it is written, painted, filmed, acted, danced, sung, witnessed, or thought about. Or shunned, denied, shamed, ridiculed, or criticized. And, regardless of whether or not it generates arousal.

There is no such thing as pornography. We need a new word.

9
Festivals

In the calendar year prior, I directed two feature films back-to-back. *Hell Town*, a ridiculous soap opera horror film, which was co-directed by Elizabeth Spear, and *El Ganzo*, a mysterious drama about the love affair between a gay black man and a straight white woman. I didn't intend to make these films back-to-back, but it happened that way.

I knew I was set to co-direct *Hell Town* over the summer. One day when I was leafing through a travel magazine, I came across an article for a small boutique hotel in Los Cabos, Mexico—Hotel *El Ganzo*. It had been designed, built and owned by the 30-year-old son of a wealthy and famous Mexican family. It featured artist residencies, and there was even a sizeable recording studio in the basement. Any musician that wanted to record an album could apply for the artist-in-residence program, and as long as they performed a concert or two on the roof, *El Ganzo* offered free room and board (and free recording studio time). The program seemed spectacular, so I emailed the hotel's owner about opportunities for filmmaker residencies.

I told him who I was and asked for free guest rooms to house my cast and crew in exchange for setting our film's story around the hotel and using *El Ganzo* as a backdrop for the film. I estimated *Hell Town* would be finished by late autumn, so perhaps a six-week shoot in January could work. It was freezing in Kansas at that time of year, so a tropical film shoot, while Kansas suffered under ice, was a welcome relief.

Within an hour, the owner replied and said, "Yeah, sounds great."

The cost they incurred could be budgeted as marketing anyhow. I was overjoyed, shaking in my shoes with excitement and couldn't believe it. I'd be escaping to work in the tropics. But then I investigated the email more closely. I had missed an important detail. The hotel owner suggested I schedule the shoot during the summer when it's off-season, when the hotel would basically be empty.

The dates mentioned left me about 10 days between wrapping *Hell Town* and then traveling to Mexico for the film shoot. I figured I could do it (emotionally and physically) so long as I was organized, and everything was planned prior to shooting *Hell Town*.

I would only need to channel my inner warrior.

Both films were produced without a hitch, and I was soon ready to embark on film festival tours for both. At the same time!

Film festivals aren't what most people think. Red-carpet glamorous moments, the kind you see in the media, are few and far between. No movie stars in gowns. No paparazzi and endless flashings of camera bulbs. No Ritz. No Carlton. None of that. So, I hired a camera crew to follow me through the tour of film festivals and document what these events are actually like.

Most often, film festivals are shabby, poorly organized, and poorly attended. A series of low-budget choices aimed at glamour. Some film festivals even have a designated "red carpet" area which consists of a backdrop strung up on a flimsy metal pole and a red square carpet measuring about eight by ten feet. Sure, you can stand on the red carpet in front of the backdrop to have someone take your picture. And when you share the photo on social media it gives the illusion that you're "on the red carpet." People might "ooh" and "ahh," thinking you are about to be interviewed by the media and overwhelmed by dozens of fans. But it's nothing like that glitzy image in real life. You'd find more reality in *Star Wars* or *Lord of the Rings*.

My friend Nicky, a hilarious and outgoing guy with a passion for film, had agreed to be the camera man for the documentary. He was built like a short muscular gymnast wrestler, so I especially liked having him around. However, he was straight, so I had to behave. I had given blowjobs to "straight" guys in the past, as one does growing up gay in Kansas. But I respected Nicky as a friend, so I wasn't going to test that boundary. Besides, I had contracted him to follow me around and film everything for the documentary. I wanted whoever held that job to be someone I considered a genuine friend.

Nicky ended up being the perfect choice.

The tour took us around the USA, to Mexico, and eventually Italy, where I would return to Venice before traveling on to Puglia.

Nicky often used hookup apps just like I did. Each time we traveled to a new city, we would each get on the apps and invite our prospective lovers to attend the screenings. Nicky on Tinder. Me on Grindr. It was charming, almost couple-like, in a strange way.

I had this dream. I got so turned on with the idea of pounding some guy in my room while Nicky was in the next room doing the same thing to some random girl. We would be two horny men, blowing off steam. Totally natural. Then, after each of us finished and sent the hookup on their way, we could compare notes and share our experiences with each other.

"He had the hottest, tightest ass," I might say.

"Dude, her mouth was on fire," he would boast.

It would be a literal blast.

But that wasn't the way life worked out. Only once did one of my potential sex buddies show up in person. It happened while we were screening *Hell Town* at the North Carolina Gay & Lesbian Film Festival. Nicky had a string of girls casually showing up in each city we visited. I may have been a bit jealous of his sex appeal. Only in North Carolina did my fantasy of mutual fucking in side-by-side rooms come to fruition. All the other times, I'd either fall asleep with a hard-on listening to Nicky pound away at some moaning, ecstatic girl, or I'd still be awake when he kicked her out. It was at times like that I had trouble controlling my thoughts about him.

Once I was on the balcony having a cigarette when Nicky came out of his room to show the nameless girl the door. He looked disappointed.

"How'd it go?" I asked.

"So-so," he said. His smooth and naked chest

glistening with droplets of sweat. *Man*, I thought, *the things I would do to that body.*

"She wouldn't blow me," he added.

"Did you cum, at least?"

"No," he said bummed.

I'd have done anything to cheer him up. I wanted to do so many things.

Instinctively, I glanced down to his shiny thin baggy gym shorts to find a clear mark of precum on the tip of a semi-hard dick, which swayed heavily back and forth as he walked over to grab a beer and take a seat nearby. I gulped. My heart pounded, sending blood coursing to my cock.

There was nothing more I wanted to do than offer him a blowjob. I wanted to grab that meaty cock through the shorts, slide them down, and suck him till he blew hot sticky cum deep in the back of my throat. But instead I immediately froze and lost all of my vocabulary skills. I felt my face flush.

"That sucks." That's all I could think to say. I felt pathetic and still so horny.

"No shit," he declared.

When we traveled to Los Cabos, Mexico, for the Los Cabos International Film Festival, the hotel put us up in one of their massive, luxurious suites complete with a terrace, an outdoor shower, and most exciting of all—one big bed. Unfortunately for me, Nicky took the sofa and was happy to. Short muscular gymnast wrestlers don't take up a lot of space.

Whilst there we met Ewan McGregor, who was being honored at the festival, and who is as attractive in real life as you might imagine.

"He's so hot," I told Nicky.

"Nah, come on," he argued.

"I'd blow him in a heartbeat."

"He's OK," Nicky agreed, "but come on, I'm at least that good-looking."

I thought to myself: *Are you trying to tell me something?*

Then it was off to Hollywood, California, for the screenings there. On my first night in town, I met several friends for happy hour. One of them brought a friend, Brian, who had been an actor in the past and was now producing shows for the Hallmark channel. Brian was tall and nearly my height, had ice-blue eyes, thick pink lips, curly brown hair, and strong broad shoulders. He was lean and twink-like, but for his height, he didn't seem too delicate or fragile. I imagined what he looked like naked and knew that I wanted him. Over the first round of drinks, we began flirting.

"You have a nice smile," he said.

I smiled and replied, "You have really beautiful eyes."

By the time our friends left, Brian and I ended up alone. The chemistry had been immediate. The tension, intense.

Soon we were back at his place.

It was his first night in a new apartment, so I picked him up and carried him over the threshold, like a newlywed bride. I didn't even have time to look around. Was it big or small? Was it clean or dirty? It didn't matter. We went in laughing. We had barely slipped inside the front door when we began making out wildly, tearing and pulling at each other. Our tongues were greedy, and I felt his hand tight on the back of my head.

He moaned when I nibbled on his ears. He reached

both hands into my pants and grabbed my ass.

I unzipped his pants and pulled out his cock. It was huge, stunning, and rock-hard. I immediately dropped to my knees and wrapped my lips around it. I twisted my mouth around his crown and made sure to use the right amount of suction and wetness. It wasn't easy and my jaw was as open as it could get.

I was nervous about my teeth scraping it. It was just so big, almost uncomfortably so. I tried to remember the techniques that 007 performed on me in the Sears parking lot. I wondered if I was performing them properly and if Brian was having a similar experience to the one I did. He stood over me and ran his fingers through my hair. His moans suggested I was doing a good job.

When he fired his load, the first shot hit the back of my throat like a cannon. I was so hard, too. I pulled my mouth off and used my hand to stroke him until he was empty. His load sprayed across the tile floor. I'd never seen so much cum.

He caught his breath, "I've never cum that quickly before... it usually takes... wow... just wow."

I smiled, licked my lips, and wiped my mouth. *Technique is key*.

I followed him into his bedroom where he apologized for not having a bed yet. There was an air mattress he needed to inflate for the night, but he wanted to cuddle. The walls were bare, too. The closets were probably empty. Normally, it would have felt a bit sad, maybe even creepy. But he was so sweet and honest and wanted affection.

So, we lay down on the floor and I spooned him. I paid attention to his breathing, listening as it calmed down. Then I suddenly noticed he had dandruff on the shoulders of his jacket. I couldn't help but examine his hair and wonder if he was aware of this or if he used conditioner. Maybe not the best time to bring that up though, I thought.

I enjoyed talking to him, so we made plans for another date the following day.

I had him meet me at my friend Susan's house, where we were introduced to a lesbian couple who had been in a band with an album released on a major record label. Brian was very affectionate in public, holding my hand, rubbing my thigh, so I reciprocated. It was lovely to feel so connected and desired.

After we left, the lesbian couple asked Susan—

"They're so cute together. How long have they been a couple?"

"Two days," Susan laughed.

Brian joined me at the screening that night. My film *El Ganzo* was playing at the Arena Cinema, and my film *Hell Town* was showing at *El Cid*, a legendary landmark built in 1905 which was D. W. Griffith's sound stage and the venue where *Birth of a Nation* was shown for the first time.

That evening with Brian was intense and magical. We went from zero to sixty in half a second, from blowjob to public appearance, and I felt no reservations. It felt so fulfilling to have a connection with someone that included actual feeling and actual care. Sex was fun, sure. But nothing beats the feeling of sex when there's genuine care involved.

I remembered Antonio's lesson from Day Four: always find something about the person you can love and love truly. I decided to pick Brian's smile and shyness.

It was beautiful to watch him move around, timidly at first but then more comfortably, and his smile was definitely something that inspired my genuine love.

I told him I loved him. For me, the L word isn't precious or heavy. I've never understood the weight some people attach to it.

It was clear to me that the feelings we both had were intense and very real. There were no false smiles, no exaggerated compliments. The chemistry was undeniable and true on some deep, fundamental level I couldn't yet understand.

When I woke up the next morning, my jaw hurt. It was at that moment that I decided that while I love sucking dick, I'd prefer a normal sized one over an enormous one any day of the week. Love still involves practicality.

After breakfast, I called and texted Brian. I left him a message about where to meet for dinner that night. I figured he was busy and would get back to me later after work, like he had the day prior.

I went to visit my friend Rob Kleiner, the music producer. He lived in an apartment in the center of Hollywood in a funny 1960s-style building. He had turned one of his bedrooms into a full-on recording studio. The singer Sia had been there to put down some vocal tracks for an album. So had other numerous music stars. I looked around the space and confessed to Rob, "I could live here."

"Good luck with that. It's a rent controlled building," he said. "No one ever leaves."

"Oh well," I thought. Perhaps someday. I knew I wanted to relocate and move out of Kansas, but I didn't know where. Maybe New York, maybe Seattle, maybe

Los Angeles.

I called Brian again that evening and left him another message.

Nothing. That hurt more than usual.

The next day, I flew home to Kansas. I went to my doctor and got tested for STIs and somehow, astonishingly, and insanely, considering all my sexual activity of the past months, I had none. Miracles do still happen.

But I did come home carrying something else. The experience with Brian had been so intense and so full of wild passion that I couldn't stop thinking about him. And I couldn't stop wondering why he hadn't responded to my calls. I called one of our mutual friends to ask if they had heard from Brian and if he was okay. Maybe he had been in a car accident, or worse. I dialed Peter.

Peter explained to me that Brian had panicked.

"You came on too strong," Peter said. "Guys normally aren't like that."

"I know," I agreed. "I'm not ordinary."

Love was apparently not something Brian was prepared to feel, to hear, or even think about.

But that's the whole point, isn't it? To have a connection with the other person that comes from a place of love so that the intimacy you share has meaning, has real substance, the kind of connection that makes life worth living. I suspect Brian is one of the people who weigh the word down with superfluous meanings attached to things like marriage.

I didn't want to marry him. I just wanted to know him, really know him. I suppose my only choice now was to appreciate what I had been able to experience with him— even if it was brief.

I had a hard time forgetting about Brian, and I felt stuck in my sorrow. I kept thinking that maybe, just maybe, there was something I could do to explain, or something that I could do to teach him, to help him. Evolve beyond whatever fear he might have. After the year I'd had, this rejection hit me hard. I was a bit dismayed. I just had to try something to hang onto the magic we experienced. But I couldn't think of any approach that would work out in my favor. The more I thought of our happy memories, the more I longed for him. The more I longed for him, the more sadness turned to anger that he had disappeared.

Suddenly, my phone rang. My mind raced to Brian, hoping it would be him. *Was I becoming obsessed?*

It wasn't Brian. It was my friend Rob Kleiner from the apartment in central Hollywood.

"I found out from the landlord someone's moving out and a one-bedroom apartment is opening up," he informed me.

"Holy shit," my mouth dropped. *Was this my moment?*

I called the landlord and told them, "I'll take it."

"Because of California law," the manager said, "you'll need to be here in person to sign the lease. We can't do it over the phone."

"Fine," I said. "I'll be there."

"You'll need to get here in thirty-six hours or..."

"Don't list it! I'll be there!"

My mind was spinning with excitement as I hung up the phone. I guess I'll be moving to Hollywood.

For the screening in Italy, I had to get Italian subtitles made for the film. Once I had them, I reached out to

Antonio in Venice to find out if he'd be willing to ensure the translation's accuracy. He agreed. We also made plans to see each other again when I was back in Venice.

Returning to Venice in autumn was as magical as arriving earlier that January. The weather had cooled down, and though the tourist hustle and bustle continued, I felt more at home. I was joined again by my friend Jennifer, who had been there earlier that year. She was one of the producers of *El Ganzo*.

Antonio met Jennifer and me for *cicchetti* and wine at one of the stops where he'd taken me on my first visit. To see him again was lovely, a portrait of Italian beauty. His eyes appeared bluer than I remembered, and his hair blonder. Probably sun-kissed from the summer months, which had passed on.

What's more, I felt no sexual attraction. None whatsoever. Although I could still find the beauty and loveliness in his spirit and in his being, I wasn't gripped by lust. My outlook on life, love, sex, and being, was lightyears from the state I'd been in when I first met him. Our original meeting, which kicked off the "Year of the Whore," was such a profound experience for me. I thought I'd feel something just as profound seeing him a second time. But it wasn't profound. It felt familiar, natural, and without weight.

Perhaps those feelings alone are, indeed, profound.

Though we explored Venice for a few days, I didn't see Antonio again during that visit. Then we were off to Tricase, in the heart of Puglia. My friend Susan, the film's leading actress, met us there, and we were joined by some of our cast and crew.

In contrast to its shabby competitors, the Salento International Film Festival is the most beautiful film festival I've ever attended. The screenings were held outdoors in the courtyard of a medieval fortress. Centuries old, piled stone surrounded us like the weight of History itself. The weather was ideal, moderate temperature and a cool breeze, perfect for outdoor viewing. The screen and the sound were executed with the finest touch. Thousands of people came dressed up in their most exquisite Italian attire. It was sublime. The award ceremony was in the center of a *piazza* with a cathedral as the backdrop. To call it extraordinary is underselling the experience.

The closing ceremony was spoken entirely in Italian. No need for a translator as we were likely the only few attending who didn't speak the language. It sounded and felt like living inside a poem, as if Fellini himself had the mic.

Eventually, in the middle of the speech, I heard the woman on stage say "*El Ganzo* de Steve Balderson," which was followed by great applause. *What?* I had no idea what she said. I looked at her and she pointed in my direction. Everyone was staring at me. I didn't know what I was supposed to do. I slowly stood up and walked toward the stage, thinking that if I wasn't supposed to be doing this, surely someone would stop me. Soon, I found myself standing on the stage front and center.

"You won," she whispered to me in English. "You won the award for Best Film!"

I took the trophy and the woman said, "Now we'll hear from the Head of the Jury, and I'll get you a translation later because it's very complicated."

My eyes began to water with joy, but I held back the tears.

The Head of the Jury made a beautiful speech. Or it

must have been, it sounded like the most gorgeous thing I've ever heard. I found out later her Italian words translated as follows:

"To the film that left our audience with tears of emotion," she stated. "For the extraordinary and poetically expressed ability to envision the recovery of one's self and the acceptance of one's inclinations, regardless of social roles, as the key to both survival and life...

"For the message of hope according to which everyone can reinvent their own existence from scratch at any time, forgetting who they were for anyone before, trusting in the other, in the unknown, and in the different. For the kindness that always comes with the absence of prejudices, and which is the core of any expression of love...

"For the pacifying role that nature takes on, whether it be stones, trees, ocean, or animals, and for the masterful synthesis of sound and images that seamlessly punctuates the whole film. Finally, for the reference to the ocean as a mother's womb for every painful and now outdated memory that faded in order to live the life that they wanted to live."

The audience applauded again, and the women turned to me.

"This is an incredible honor," I spoke into the microphone. My eyes were to the point at which tears would drop at any second. I couldn't hold back much more.

"We hope it's just the beginning for you," she said.

"*Grazie mille,*" I said, eyes watering, finally letting loose, feeling the circle complete.

"*Grazie mille.*"

10

Epilogue: Westward

I had less than twenty-four hours to decide what, of all the furniture and things that filled my five-bedroom house, would be moved into a tiny one-bedroom apartment in Hollywood. I knew I couldn't park a big pickup truck easily anywhere in LA, so I traded vehicles with my dad. He took my truck, and I took his small SUV. Once I had some essentials packed in the SUV, I walked through the enormous house and put everything that was to be moved into the dining room. The moving company was instructed to take everything that was in the kitchen, the dining room, and master bedroom. The rest of the furniture in other rooms could be put into storage or divvied up for safe keeping by my family.

The morning of departure came, and I woke up early. It was a crisp winter's day and there was frost in the air. It had been exactly a year since I returned from Italy with a newfound sense of identity, which in part, came from learning all the sensual pleasures a human body can experience.

As I headed to the car, I felt an overwhelming sense of excitement, thrill, hope and adventure. I turned around one last time to look at my house—the place I had built as a home for my future, which was no longer a possibility.

"Thank you, *Pipistrello*," I whispered to the house and my eyes suddenly flooded with tears. I choked out a barely audible, "It's been fun."

I climbed into the car without looking back and drove toward the interstate. I sobbed so relentlessly I had trouble seeing. I kept crying until I reached halfway across Kansas.

I intentionally avoided listening to the radio. I didn't need the lyrics of any songs to persuade my mind into thinking things I didn't truly feel. I wanted to appreciate the feeling of the moment as I was living and experiencing it. I relished the silence and stillness. Music is often taken for granted, especially in film, but on that note, so is silence. The only thing I heard was the white noise of the car, the tires on the road, and the wind passing by outside.

The sounds calmed my mind and eventually the tears stopped falling. I didn't utter a word other than to order food when I stopped for a bite to eat. I spent the night in a hotel near the highway and woke again early the next morning to get back on the road.

A strong sensation washed over me as I drove through New Mexico. I had driven from Kansas to Los Angeles many times while attending film school at California Institute of the Arts. I knew the route by heart. Soon, I'd be crossing the border into Arizona, and coming up after that is the Painted Desert. I recalled my excitement each time I saw it. The area is a desert landscape with colors so vibrant they touch the soul and a spiritual energy that is both distinct but hard to describe. Layers of sandstone, clay, and volcanic soil in reds, golds, and lavender.

Today, the anticipation of driving through the Painted Desert felt different. It felt like the very first time approaching it. Each roadside marker passed me, and the untamed landscape crept closer with a heightened exposure. A brighter light.

As I entered the Painted Desert, my mother's advice echoed across the vast landscape and I found myself smiling. I had indeed learned to walk again. My resurrection happened at that instant. I experienced my body and spirit filling up with a gold, warm, and bright light. Restoration. A liquid oneness connecting me to the mountains, the sky, to nature in all directions. This place, this point in the Universe, was exactly where I should have been for what I had been through. Connecting me to all people, each of us to one another, and to the whole world, our planet, to the cosmos—and suddenly, a shockwave fired in all directions so bold and powerful it could rival the force of a supernova. The Universe had signaled, and this was my Big Bang, this was my Genesis, this was, while the final chapter in one act of my life, the beginning I needed.

In the exhilaration of that moment, and with so much of the world left to explore and experience, I knew that I would sell my house and never return.

From then on, with every mile that passed, I felt a weight being lifted. There was an enormous sense of letting go, of dissolving, melting, and forgiving.

Each mile marker, exit, or other car that I passed, I felt a force getting stronger. A sense of awareness of the future, a new embrace, new strength, curiosity, and awe. A new age of personal exploration set to touch down on an unknown but exciting soil.

I felt my inner warrior spirit igniting.

YEAR OF THE WHORE

STEVE BALDERSON

ABOUT THE AUTHOR

Preeminent film critic Roger Ebert gave Steve's film *Firecracker*, starring Karen Black and Mike Patton, a Special Jury Award on his annual Best Films of the Year list. His first film *Pep Squad* premiered at the Cannes Film Festival and became a 90s cult classic. The U.S. Library of Congress selected his film *The Casserole Club*, starring Kevin Richardson of the Backstreet Boys, for its permanent collection. Steve ranks #47 on the IMDb's Top 100 Gay and Lesbian Directors working today. His first book, *"Filmmaking Confidential,"* debuted as an Amazon and Audible best-seller. He is a contributor to The Advocate and MovieMaker magazines and has been a guest lecturer at the University of California Los Angeles (UCLA).

BOOKS BY THE AUTHOR

"Filmmaking Confidential"
(2020, Dikenga Books)

"How to Find Investors"
(2021, Dikenga Books)

"The Master Plan"
(2022, Dikenga Books)

"PHONE SEX"
(2021, Dikenga Books)

https://linktr.ee/balderson
www.SteveBalderson.com
www.DIKENGA.com

Made in the USA
Monee, IL
01 June 2023

35075071R00069